Rails Through Lakeland

Volume 2

A view of the industrial western end of the route, on which its foundations and early prosperity had been built. A 'Cauliflower' 0-6-0 is rounding the sharply curving approach to Derwent Junction, Workington, with a short freight train from Cockermouth. The locomotive is carrying a shedplate bearing the 12D code – used by Workington in LMS days after 1935. By 1985 the terraced cottages in the background had disappeared, along with the railway, which closed between Keswick and Workington in 1966. Note on the left the signal on the single track to the docks that crossed the coastal main line. *Richard L. Pattinson/CRA*

Rails Through Lakeland

An illustrated history of the Workington-Cockermouth-Keswick-Penrith Railway, 1847-1972

Volume 2
Traffic and operation

Harold D. Bowtell

·RAILWAY HERITAGE·
from
The NOSTALGIA Collection

First published in a single volume as *Rails Through Lakeland* in 1989
Reprinted 1991
New two-volume paperback edition:
Volume 1 first published 1999
Volume 2 first published 2000

British Library Cataloguing in Publication Data

A catalogue record for this book is available from the British Library.

ISBN 1 85794 128 4

Silver Link Publishing Ltd
The Trundle
Ringstead Road
Great Addington
Kettering
Northants NN14 4BW

Tel/Fax: 01536 330588
email: sales@slinkp-p.demon.co.uk

Printed and bound in Great Britain

Abbreviations

C&WJnR	Cleator & Workington Junction Railway
C&WR	Cockermouth & Workington Railway
CKPR	Cockermouth, Keswick & Penrith Railway
LMS	London Midland & Scottish Railway
LNWR	London & North Western Railway
M&CR	Maryport & Carlisle Railway
MO	Mondays only
NER	North Eastern Railway
S&DR	Stockton & Darlington Railway
SO	Saturdays only
SX	Saturdays excepted
WC&ER	Whitehaven, Cleator & Egremont Railway
wef	with effect from
WJnR	Whitehaven Junction Railway

Contents

COCKERMOUTH, KESWICK & PENRITH RAILWAY.

PILOTMAN'S TICKET.

To be used in accordance with Rule 25 of the Regulations for Train Signalling on Single Lines of Railway worked on the Electric Train Tablet Block System.

*Train No.*_____

To the GUARD and ENGINE DRIVER.

You are authorised to proceed from

_____ *to* _____

PILOTMAN FOLLOWING.

*Signature of Pilotman,*_____

*Date,*_____18   [OVER.]

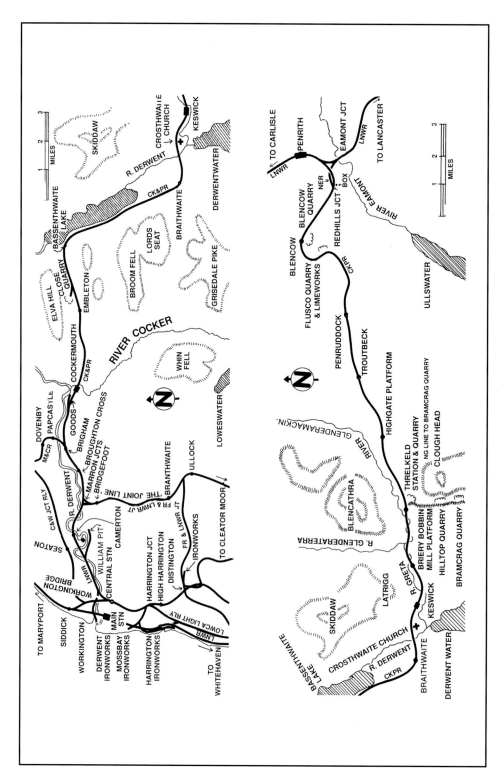

The Workington-Cockermouth-Keswick-Penrith Railway

1. Mineral and industrial traffic

The economic seesaw, 1866-1914

The iron and steel industry developed with incredible speed in Britain during the third quarter of the 19th century – as witnessed by the creation of Barrow-in-Furness and Middlesbrough and all they stood for. Even so, the industry was to have a very chequered career, owing to its susceptibility to 'boom and slump' from local and, even more, overseas causes.

The works that figured in West Cumberland, with blast furnaces and thus calling for iron ore, limestone and coke, are listed in the table overleaf. It will be seen that their early development was mostly in the 1860s and 1870s. During these decades,

emphasis was on the export of pig iron produced in West Cumberland's blast furnaces, particularly across country to Teesside and the East Coast ports and to the earlier Bessemer steel manufacturing companies in the Sheffield district. As steel-making became established at the more technically advanced Cumbrian works, the pig iron was required for use in their own steelworks and their products were chiefly of steel, notably rails for the world's railways, manufactured and rolled at Workington. The table thus provides a pointer to the recipients of west-bound coke brought from County Durham by way of the CKPR and to the sources in West Cumberland of east-bound

A down goods leaves Workington Bridge station in LMS days, bound for Derwent Junction, hauled by an LNWR 'Cauliflower' 0-6-0. Industrial activity in West Cumbria was the spur for the construction of the C&WR and CKPR. *Richard L. Pattinson/CRA*

Iron works of West Cumberland having blast furnaces producing pig iron and demanding coke

1. Works located south of the railway route from Cockermouth to Derwent Junction and Workington. These were most likely to import coke from County Durham by way of the Stainmore route and Keswick.

Title	First production (circa)	Substantially enlarged (circa)	Decline commenced (circa)	Final demise
Cleator Moor	1841	1862-82	1920	1929
Harrington	1857	1872-82	1909	1926
Lonsdale (Whitehaven)	1872	1873-83	1890s	1902
Moss Bay (Workington)	1872	1872-77, 1934, 1949-66	1974	1981* (Steel also made from 1877)
Derwent (Workington)	1873	1873-79, 1883, 1893-97	1974	1981* (Steel also made from 1883)
Parton	1874	Soon in decline		1889
Distington	1878	1878-82	1921	1922

*The creation of the Workington Iron & Steel Co Ltd in 1910 led to most of future investment being in the adjoining Moss Bay and Derwent works, with their progressively closer working and virtual integration from 1934.

After cessation of production of iron and steel in 1981, the rail rolling mills continued to operate but using steel from Teesside.

In general, substantial production of pig iron was achieved by circa 1880, with Cleator Moor, Harrington, Distington, Moss Bay and Derwent works continuing into the 20th century and only the progressively merging Moss Bay and Derwent works surviving effectively beyond 1920. These were the two iron and steel works in West Cumberland (apart from limited production at one works mentioned below) and have rolled steel rails ever since the 1877-83 period.

2. Works located north of the River Derwent, being those most likely to import coke from the Durham coalfield by way of Carlisle.

Title	First production	Substantially enlarged	Decline commenced	Final demise
Oldside (Workington)	1841	1879-80	progressive	1930
West Cumberland (Workington)	1862	1862-72, 1899	1885	1900 (Steel from 1870-72 until demise)
Lowther (Workington)	1873	1873-82	1897-1905	1911
Maryport	1868	1868-82	1883	1892
Solway (at Maryport)	1871	1871-72	1921	1927 (or earlier)

traffic (until about the end of the 1870s) in pig iron and (later) steel in various forms, rails in particular.

As early as 1866 the CKPR Board was complaining to Euston that pig iron was being sent from Workington to Sheffield by way of the Furness Railway (FR) to Carnforth and the LNWR onwards to Preston (and thence maybe by the Lancashire & Yorkshire Railway (LYR) via Blackburn, Copy Pit, Huddersfield and Penistone, finally via the Manchester, Sheffield & Lincolnshire Railway (MSLR) into Sheffield). The CKPR contended that the LNWR's agreement on 'shortest routes' implied use of the CKPR and the LNWR's own Ingleton branch, to reach the Midland Railway (MR), which would provide a direct route, from Ingleton via Leeds to Sheffield. In April 1867 LNWR General Manager William Cawkwell was at last writing, to say that routing to such destinations as Sheffield via the CKPR and Ingleton 'and so off their LNWR line' was never contemplated, the alternatives being the CKPR, Shap and Preston or by the Furness Railway and Preston. Methinks he protesteth too much! The underlying reason would be to maximise LNWR revenue-earning train mileage and collaborate with friendly companies such as the NER or LYR, but keeping the MR out of the picture at all costs. A compromise formula was arrived at in June 1867.

Also in 1866 the CKPR failed to secure a share in iron ore traffic from West Cumberland to Consett ironworks; it was presumably lost to the LNWR, M&CR and NER, via Carlisle. In 1868 the NER declined to reduce its rates for conveying coke on the axis from Durham to Stainmore, the CKPR and West Cumberland, saying that the lower rates in force between Durham, Stainmore, Tebay and Barrow dated from agreements between the S&DR and Schneider & Company, ironmasters at Barrow. In July 1868 the LNWR sought, by rate adjustments, to influence the routing of traffic in pig iron coming off the Joint Line and bound via the CKPR for Hull, Goole and Grimsby. Presumably at that date the pig iron originated from Cleator Moor and was bound for shipment to the continent; it is said that

Prussia provided a market for Cumbrian pig iron, used in making cannon, until the time of the Franco-Prussian war of 1870.

Further evidence of the existence of iron ore traffic eastward via CKPR metals and the NER Stainmore route – but also of slump – was provided when bad debts had to be written off. These resulted from the failure of the South Cleveland Iron Works Company Ltd (1875) and the Rosedale & Ferryhill Iron Company (1879). In the first case the ore had moved from the Joint Line to Glaisdale furnaces, situated beside the NER's delightful Esk Valley line. In the latter, it would be ore transported to Ferryhill, north of Darlington on the Anglo-Scottish East Coast Main Line. The late 1870s were notable for depressed traffics in coke westward and iron ore eastward, and reduced rates for their conveyance. Import of Spanish ore from 1871, on an increasing scale, progressively ended the eastbound traffic in West Cumberland ore via Keswick. Nationally, January 1879 witnessed a cut in the bank rate, doubtless aimed at stimulating reluctant exports, while locally a squeeze was applied to wages by the CKPR, mainly in the traffic and permanent way departments.

In 1880-83 the tale was different. West Cumberland achieved its maximum output of iron ore during the years 1881-83. Already, in February 1880, the NER had requested night opening of the CKPR to accommodate the increased and heavy coke traffic westbound over the line and to eliminate the working of 'double trains' – that is, double loads with two engines – which the NER was finding 'dangerous and productive of delays'. The CKPR agreed promptly, in February 1880, and a limited period of night opening was instituted. A similar request was made and agreed in December 1881, the night working commencing from 1 January 1882. Again, wef March 1883, night working was introduced, to meet pressure of peak coke traffic. These spells would put great pressure on the staff of the CKPR, especially the signalmen and other traffic men, who would find themselves working 12-hour turns of duty.

From 1883, slump set in with a vengeance and continued for several years. By January

This dramatic scene illustrates vehicles of a 'double' coke train from Mid Durham to West Cumberland on 1 November 1900. The wagons (tare weight 6 tons 15 cwt to 6 tons 19 cwt, according to precise type) had a carrying capacity of 10½ tons and were built specifically for the traffic from former S&DR territory – note the NER lettering 'Central Division and West Cumberland'. The rear van, with double veranda and large central 'birdcage', is of a genuine S&DR design, while the van with an end 'birdcage' was designed by the NER to diagram V1. The pile-up occurred at Blencow during the period of widening works between Redhills and Blencow; there was a derailment or run-back of a westbound loaded train on the newly formed embankment. *Ian G. Sadler collection*

1884 the ironmasters of West Cumberland were combining to press the railway companies for reduced coke rates from the Durham and Newcastle districts; the NER, M&CR and CKPR agreed, while the LNWR, grudgingly, offered only a partial concession. Even at Threlkeld quarries, whose output was granite, not limestone for blast furnaces, poor trade was evident in their dealings with the railway in 1883 and 1884. It is recorded that nearly half the furnaces in West Cumberland were 'out of blast' by August 1886.

In sympathy with decreased levels of trade, the CKPR's annual rate of dividend declared showed fluctuations in the range 3% to 6% during most of the 1870s, falling to 2½% at the close of the last half-year of 1879 but rising to 5-6¾% in the period 1880-81. This was accompanied by stirrings for increased salaries among the company's staff. Dividends were notably low in 1886, up again in 1889 and also for a year or two after, while the years 1888-89 witnessed the nearest approach to 1881-82 levels of production from the Cumberland iron ore mines. In the winter of 1890-91, the LNWR offered to buy the CKPR, at 5% on the ordinary capital; the Board hesitated and the propitious moment passed, never to recur. A coal strike in 1892 depressed trade, and the import of coke from County Durham to West Cumberland was suspended for some months.

In the new century (January 1904) the ironmasters (now formally represented by the West Cumberland Ironmasters' Association,

Representative consignment notes of the CKPR period, 1874-1897. From the top, they are Charles Ray's horse, in horsebox, sent from Braithwaite to Euston by day service on 19 March 1875 (presumably the horse travelled by passenger train on the CKPR but possibly by horse-and-carriage train on the main line, at a fare of 6s 11d); 10 boxes of kippers sent from the north via Penrith to Keswick on 19 January 1897; and a dog, conveyed from Embleton to Penrith on 12 May 1874 for 1 shilling. J. M. Hammond collection

with F. W. Jackson as Secretary) sought reduced through rates for coke from the Newcastle and Durham districts to the iron furnaces of West Cumberland. A meeting between the Association and the railway companies at Carlisle in March 1904 was inconclusive. In May the CKPR agreed with Mr Burtt, the NER Traffic Manager, to allow a rebate of 10% off the through coke rates for the period 1 April-31 December 1904. The interested companies met at Euston on 2 August 1904, when the agreement was ratified; it was subsequently extended to 31 March 1905, then 30 June 1905. Then, in August 1905, the railway companies again met at Euston and agreed a 'permanent' allowance off Durham-West Coast coke rates: 5d off 5 shillings and under, and 6d off rates over 5 shillings per ton. The companies shared the sacrifice proportionally, according to their coke train mileages.

In 1910 Mr T. Ainsworth, of the Cleator Moor Company, with extensive iron ore mining interests, sought from the CKPR a reduction in the eastward rates for iron ore from Eskett Junction (on the Joint Line) to Middlesbrough. The CKPR was prepared to accept 6 shillings per ton on a confirmed order of 10,000 tons if the LNWR and NER would agree – the outcome is not recorded.

The members of the CKPR Board noted, in May 1911, that revenue 'is in a low condition'. They each agreed to deduct £100 per annum from their fees while this continued and

Coke conveyed by rail from collieries in NE England to West Cumberland

The table begins with the high-production period of 1888-89, when the all-time peak of 1881-82 in the West Cumberland iron and steel industry was most nearly approached. It ignores the substantial tonnages travelling by Stainmore and Tebay to Carnforth and Furness ironworks.

Year	Tonnage via Keswick	Number of trains daily via Keswick (approx)	Tonnage via Carlisle
1887-89	228,436*	4	483,510*
1890-94	185,173*	3-4	323,272*
1895-99	200,853*	4	397,620*
1900	219,334	4 (+1 conditional)	462,616
1901	192,388	3	422,262
1902	201,622	3	450,861
1903	156,779	2	438,880
1904	133,753	2	411,362
1905	109,262	2	489,658
1906	121,603	2	552,976
1907	123,818	2	589,730
1908	96,207	1-2	384,668
1909	116,482	2	389,079
1910	74,489	1	385,523
1911	20,852	1	232,624
1912	17,541	1 (and not daily)	165,549
1913	16,422	1 (conditional)	215,656
1914	27,088	1	110,765
1915	61,440	1-2	147,388
1916	93,116	2	196,736
1917	74,637	1-2	290,424
1918	111,935	2 (or 1 + 2 conditional)	289,087
1920		2	
1921		1 (+ 1 conditional)	
1922		1 (+ 1 conditional)	
1925		2 (conditional)	

*Indicates yearly averages during 1887-1899

decided on various redefinitions of staff duties; one might describe this as 'cheese-paring'. Thus the junior fencer and Mr Black, the quarryman at the company's Flusco ballast quarry, were to be given notice, likewise (wef from the end of September 1911) William Richardson, the company's canvasser. The gardener's pay was to be cut to the rate of £40 a year after the end of October. The painting staff was to be reduced to one man and an apprentice from the spring of 1912, and major painting work was to be entrusted to contractors.

There was a countrywide railway strike on 18-19 August 1911 and a miners' strike in March-April 1912. However, from August 1912, and during the years 1912-14, progressive increases of pay for staff, negotiated sectionally, reflected better trade and traffics. Some rates increased by 4% from 1 July 1913 – although the company's declared dividends were minimal.

When examining the accompanying table it is interesting to note that the figures for 1892-93 are curtailed by the coal strike of 1892 but increased by traffic diversion from the Furness Railway for some months after the subsidence disaster at Lindal of October 1892. Numbers of trains quoted (daily average) assume that during the period covered by the table the traffic via Keswick was usually made up by the NER/LNER in 'double loads'. The use of two NER locomotives on each train of coke, with corresponding balancing workings, as between Kirkby Stephen and Cockermouth, is the pattern generally recalled or passed down the generations. The figures have been deduced from the tonnages but are also supported by spot-checking of working timetables.

It is also interesting to observe that the tonnage routed via Carlisle was usually double that sent via Keswick between the mid-1880s and 1902, the ratio moving to three and four times and, by 1911-13, to more like ten times. There was a temporary recovery in Keswick route traffic during the war of 1914-18 and for a year or two afterwards. The Keswick traffic (via the Redhills link) became intermittent and ended in 1926. However, there is evidence of a revival in 1928-29; McGowan Gradon referred to reversal at Penrith in 1928

and D. S. Barrie photographed a double-headed coke train near Eamont Junction in, seemingly, 1929.

Coking of coal at West Cumberland sites for use in the district's iron industry only commenced on a significant scale in about 1908, but it quickly became the policy of the Workington Iron & Steel Co Ltd, from its formation in 1909-10, to be self-sufficient in coke from plants at selected collieries in West Cumberland and from batteries of ovens at the integrated iron and steel works at Moss Bay/Derwent, from 1936: this was the factor that finally killed the traffic.

While the accompanying table and notes give a good indication of the scale of the coke traffic that passed over the CKPR from the 1880s until the traffic faded away in the early and mid-1920s, the question of how this traffic was handled west of Cockermouth is obscure. The LNWR clearly treated this as 'trip' working and did not include it in its working timetables. The company would have an incentive to run, using its own locomotives and train crews, via Derwent Junction through to the ironworks, but there are indications that the 'Johnny-come-lately' Cleator & Workington Junction Railway contrived to take over much of the coke at Workington Bridge and run it over its own metals to Harrington Junction and thence by its branch lines to Moss Bay and Derwent Works, as well as over the length of the C&WJnR 'main line' to Cleator Moor works. In addition, some of the coke coming via Carlisle and the M&CR was probably routed via Linefoot to Harrington Junction.

Basic freight services in the early 20th century

Beyond the important conveyance of coke between West Durham and West Cumberland – and some balancing eastward movement of iron ore and pig iron – there was, in general, little use in peacetime of the CKPR route for through transit, and no services that could be styled express goods trains. The LNWR term 'fast goods' was a misnomer when applied to a CKPR working – one might kindly say that it was relative rather than definitive!

From the LNWR/CKPR of the early 20th century to the combined LMS of the 1920s, the pattern of freight trains was remarkably constant, and can be summarised thus:

Up direction, Cockermouth-Keswick-Penrith

1 Morning goods, originating at Cockermouth Yard and leaving the Junction at 9.40am (1906), 10.25am (1918), 9.20am (1921) or 9.55am (1925) bound, with many calls, for Penrith, where it was due variously between 12.55pm and 2.35pm, according to the schedule in force. Arrival intermediately at Keswick ranged between 10.50am and 12.05pm, but the stay there was never booked (in tables studied) to exceed 20 minutes, implying that traffic collected there had already been assembled and placed ready for attachment.

2 Midday 'fast goods' from Workington, leaving or passing the 'Main' station at 12 noon to 2.55pm (timings varying down the years) and making calls through to Penrith, due 4.20pm in early century, but by 1914 and after terminating at Keswick, around 4.30-5.30pm.

Among calls, that at Cockermouth Junction (and Yard) was usually allowed about 1 hour.

3 Early evening local goods train from Keswick (or Threlkeld) to Penrith, with intermediate calls. Until at least 1918 the light engine (or engine and van) left Keswick at 5.55pm (6.40pm by 1918) for Threlkeld and the goods was booked to start at Threlkeld at 6.20pm (7.07pm by 1918) for Penrith (due 7.45pm). In 1921, and into LMS days, the goods officially originated at Keswick (at 6.00pm) with calls to Penrith (due around 7.40pm).

There were also workings that, while booked daily, were clearly provided to offer relief from overloading of those already tabulated:

1 From 1914, or rather earlier, a 'teatime' goods was booked from Threlkeld (departing variously at 4.40pm, 4.45pm and 4.50pm) to Penrith (due 6.00pm or thereabouts). Note that by 1921 onwards the early evening goods was starting with a load from Keswick – as, one suspects, it may well have done informally even before that – barely pausing at

A modest eastbound (up) goods train comprising three wagons and a standard BR 20-ton brake-van leaves Keswick on 14 August 1950 behind a 'Cauliflower' of 12C (Penrith) shed. *Neville Fields*

Threlkeld. Nevertheless, in the 1920s and the earlier 1930s there were periods when Threlkeld quarries loaded the available 18-inch goods ('Cauliflower') 0-6-0 engine to its maximum of about 11 wagons of granite for the climb from Threlkeld to Troutbeck. Alternatively, the locomotive would often make two trips with loads up the bank to Troutbeck, finally assembling its train there for the onward run to Penrith.

2 In the last year of the war (1918), a 'mineral train' was booked from Workington at 9.25am, with a conditional call at Close Quarry Siding and brief stops at Bassenthwaite Lake and Keswick, to Redhills Junction and onwards, evidently using the NER Redhills cut-off to reach Ingleton. While this train could have continued to a destination on the Midland Railway, it could also have made connection with Ingleton Quarries or the New Ingleton Colliery, the latter developing, with rail connection, from about 1912 and operating until 1925.

3 In the 1920s a 10.50am Workington-Keswick (due 2.6pm) goods appears, calling at Brigham (for 30 minutes), Cockermouth Junction (1 hour) and briefly onwards, including Close Quarry Siding.

Some of the Monday and Saturday times differed from those listed here, but the 'pattern' was little different.

Down direction, Penrith-Keswick-Cockermouth
1 'The mail': this was the early goods, leaving Penrith at times between 5.30am and 5.45am, for Cockermouth Junction (reached variously between 8.38am and 9.15am) and conveying mails as far as Keswick. Many of its calls were brief but it spent about an hour at Keswick, detaching a van containing newspapers, and wagon-load traffic, as well as goods for early delivery around the town and environs, while empties were placed by the engine, ready for an up working.

2 'The Keswick goods': the mid-morning local goods, leaving Penrith Yard at between 10.40am and 11.15am and due into Keswick between 1.00pm and 1.20pm, with fairly brief roadside calls except at Threlkeld, where typically a half-hour was allowed for traffic purposes, although this was liable to be extended on Saturdays to enable the engine and guard to take the quarry-workers' passenger train from Threlkeld to Keswick, and return 'light' to complete their duties before continuing with the goods to Keswick. This goods train was scheduled to call at Briery Siding to attach and detach traffic, at dates as far apart as 1906 and 1925, although in 1914 that service was performed by the preceding NER mineral train.

3 The afternoon Keswick goods and its onward connection westward: in 1906 this was a through working, at 5.20pm ex-Penrith, to Cockermouth Goods (due 8.40pm), with calls on the road, including 6.55-7.20pm at Keswick. In the years 1914-18 it left Penrith about 3.40pm or 3.55pm, but the departure time crept forward over the years, to 2.40pm by 1925. The intermediate calls progressively lengthened, and booked arrival at Keswick fell back progressively from 5.15pm towards 5.40pm. The onwards goods train left Keswick at times between 6.45pm and 7.50pm and made various calls to Cockermouth Junction, inclusive, then ran fast to Workington, due between 9.00pm and 9.30pm or thereabouts. In 1921, maybe generally, it was the train used to convey coal for Cockermouth line stations west of Keswick.

By early LMS days an additional service was scheduled at 3.08pm daily, from Keswick to Workington (5.40pm), with traffic calls that included about 30 minutes at both Cockermouth Junction and Brigham.

Subsidiary freight services in the early 20th century
On the CKPR line proper the odd 'short' working was run from Keswick to Threlkeld and/or Troutbeck; for example, the 2.15pm Troutbeck goods was booked daily for many years in the period 1914-25 (at least), as well as 'conditional' trips. Calls at Briery Siding by the down goods or mineral trains have already

been mentioned, but additionally 'trip' workings from Keswick to the Siding and back have also been recalled.

At the western end, on the C&WR line, the Monday cattle market at Cockermouth was a great source of traffic; note the extensive cattle pen facilities provided adjoining Cockermouth passenger station. The M&CR's link at Brigham to such places as Aspatria and Wigton and its running powers to and from Cockermouth produced both general goods and livestock traffic, with Mondays the busiest day by far. There was clear cause for congestion on the single line between Cockermouth Junction and the passenger station, which was also traversed by M&CR passenger shuttle trains, as well as the basic Workington-Keswick passenger and freight service, not forgetting the fluctuating pattern of NER through mineral working.

There were typically two early morning trains from Workington to Cockermouth Goods, one being a mineral train from Derwent Iron Works, while on Mondays cattle trains had to run from Workington to Cockermouth passenger station and its yard. In early century a 'mixed' train ran from Moor Row by the Joint Line to Marron Junction and was liable to be combined there with the 8.10am goods from Workington, which thus conveyed passengers and freight onwards. Accordingly it had to run through to Cockermouth passenger station. In the same period, the down working of the goods and mineral train from Cockermouth Goods to Workington was at 11.00am and it had to detach coke (doubtless derived via the NER and CKPR from Durham) at Marron Junction for the LNWR's 11.25am mineral duty to Ullock and Distington Iron Works. Clearly, the LNWR was maintaining its connection with Distington Works, against potential competition from the newer route created by the C&WJnR. Another working by the (former) LNWR/FR Joint Line was evident in 1925; this was 7.40am MO express goods from Drigg (Furness line) to Cockermouth Passenger (due 10.50am), with return at 4.07pm MO Cockermouth Passenger-Drigg, angled at cattle traffic from/to Egremont and neighbourhood.

Papcastle Quarry was served by a shuttle working from Brigham, formed by the engine and brake of an up C&WR goods, a member of Brigham station staff accompanying the trip. The working continued nearly to the end of the LMS era. In earlier times a mineral train was run as required at 9.55am from Workington to Papcastle, returning at 12.35pm from Papcastle.

A relic of early C&WR days survived (just) in 1906, when the 'conditional' train from Papcastle to Workington was booked at Marron Junction from 1.48pm to 3.10pm. It shunted at Lowther Pit from 2.00pm to 2.55pm, but this had declined with the fading fortunes of the pit by 1914.

William Pit Sidings, between Workington Bridge and Camerton stations, provided the junction and exchange point for the colliery branch line, worked by the Allerdale Coal Company's locomotives. This signal box figured in calls between Cockermouth and Workington, also in a specific 'trip' working from/to Workington. The pit dated from the 1880s and produced traffic until 1959, with subsequent dismantling of the colliery and branch line in 1961.

One may also mention traffic between the Joint Line and Workington via Marron Junction and Derwent Junction, associated with the many private sidings and branch lines served – the output of iron ore mines being for many years the main source of traffic from the Joint Line's territory. A latter-day traffic was limestone from the United Steel Company's Rowrah Hall quarries, routed via Marron to the iron and steel works at Moss Bay. This operated from August 1938 until (probably) November 1953, when the old Joint route effectively ceased to be used – apart from the northward passage on 5 September 1954 of the 'West Cumberland Rail Tour' train of the Stephenson Locomotive Society and the Manchester Locomotive Society.

Freight in later times

The disappearance of the Durham-West Cumberland coke traffic, which essentially ended in 1926, has been described. The 'great depression' of the early 1930s, following the

Wall Street financial 'crash' of 1929, was particularly severe in West Cumberland and caused the final demise of much long-established industry. This was obviously detrimental to traffic associated with Maryport and Workington and their immediate hinterland. The former 'Joint Line' declined with its industries and with the developing hold of motor traffic on goods and livestock movements. The Bullgill-Brigham (formerly M&CR) line closed from 29 April 1935, finally ending the Monday mornings of bustle at Cockermouth passenger station and its cattle sidings.

However, the LMS did its best and kept up much of the 'traditional' pattern of freight on the CKPR route, helped by virtual removal of competition in the war years from 1939 to 1945 and for a very few years afterwards. ASLEF (the footplatemen's trade union) called its incredibly foolhardy strike from 29 May to 14 June 1955 with the result that many freight and mineral traffics were lost for ever by the railways.

BR's Modernisation Plan of March 1955 received close scrutiny and generally favourable endorsement from a powerful parliamentary committee. However, the Macmillan Government chose to ignore this and appointed Richard Beeching and Ivan Stedteford from outside industry to make a quite different appraisal. From this emerged the infamous 'Beeching plan' of 1963, and the subsequent decision wilfully to throw to the wolves almost all of BR's then still extensive freight traffic – an objective achieved with great rapidity. The CKPR stations at that time retaining layout, accommodation and staff for handling freight traffic were: Brigham, Cockermouth Goods, Bassenthwaite Lake, Braithwaite, Keswick, Threlkeld, Troutbeck, Penruddock and Blencow. Goods facilities were withdrawn from all stations at a stroke, with effect from 1 June 1964. Only Flusco and Blencow quarries, at the eastern end of the line, retained connections by which to despatch stone by rail – until 16 June 1972.

The years 1952-55 may be said to represent the final era of post-war freight working, before disaster overtook it. The basic

provisions of that period on the Keswick route comprised:

Up

7.25am: daily (becoming 7.18am) Workington-Cockermouth Junction (8.00am) and Yard.

9.25am: Cockermouth Junction-Penrith Goods, due 2.20pm (later 1.05pm) with calls including Keswick (10.47-11.26am), Threlkeld (11.38-11.52am), Penruddock (12.15-12.55pm), Blencow (1.07-2.05pm in 1952, but omitted by 1955).

1.05pm: SX Workington-Keswick goods, due 4.52pm, with calls.

5.15pm: daily (4.55pm SX by 1955) Keswick-Penrith goods, due at 6.48pm (6.15pm SX by 1955), with only a few calls.

Down

6.10am: SX Penrith-Cockermouth Junction 'goods and mails', due 8.46am, with various brief calls but typically at Keswick 7.01-7.54am. SO in 1952, it ran only between Keswick and Cockermouth, at the same times, with no mails conveyed – and in 1955 it ran daily throughout from Penrith, but no mails are mentioned.

1.51pm: daily (SX by 1955) Penrith-Keswick goods, due 4.22pm, with calls.

6.25pm: SX (6.14pm SX by 1955) Keswick-Workington goods, with some calls.

Thus, taking account also of the 11.44am (see below), there were effectively two goods workings each way over the whole route, to be compared with, in general, three in times past. Subsidiary workings of 1952-55 were:

9.00am: Cockermouth Junction-Cockermouth Passenger goods train.

9.45am: Cockermouth Passenger-Cockermouth Junction, calling Gas Works Siding 9.48-10.00am.

11.44am: Cockermouth Junction-Workington, due 1.13pm, with calls including William Pit (and it was preceded by a 'trip' working, William Pit-Workington). (The pit closed in March 1959.)

Two afternoon SX 'conditional' workings (one for 1955) for engine and brake between

On 26 July 1963 a Keswick-Penrith goods train, including sheeted limestone wagons, drifts down the gradient off the CKPR line near No 1 signal box, converging directly with the down West Coast Main Line, bound for Penrith yard. *Derek Cross*

Workington and Cockermouth passenger station were balanced by conditional freight paths at 4.00pm (not in 1955) and 5.16pm from Cockermouth Passenger station to Workington Dock and Maryport (Workington Main by 1955).

The junction for the 'Joint Line' figured with one trip (SX) in September 1952 (vanished by 1955), namely Workington 2.55pm to Marron Junction, due 3.35pm, with empties, calling at William Pit Sidings. Its return was from Marron Junction (3.45pm) to Workington (due 4.20pm), calling once more at William Pit Sidings.

At the eastern end, the continued significant stone traffic from the private quarry connections at Blencow and Flusco called for a 'trip' working, namely 10.42am daily (10.37am in 1955) from Penrith to Blencow (11.00-11.45am) and Flusco Siding (due 11.50am), returning at 12.32pm to Penrith (booked arrival 1.20pm).

2. Passenger traffic

C&WR passenger trains, 1847-1866

The passenger trains introduced between Cockermouth and Workington (8½ miles), from 28 April 1847, assumed a fairly logical pattern by the end of that summer:

Cockermouth: depart for Workington
   6.55am, 10.10am, 2.10pm, 5.50pm, 6.30pm
Workington: depart for Cockermouth
   8.10am, 10.55am, 2.55pm, 6.35pm, 7.30pm

Thus there were five trips each way on weekdays, with four each way on Sundays. Calls were at Brigham, Broughton and Camerton, and the fare throughout was 1s 6d, 1s and 8d for 1st, 2nd and 3rd Class single tickets. Clearly, one passenger engine and set of carriages could cover this timetable.

In 1850 weekdays trains were (seemingly) unbalanced, with four advertised from Cockermouth but six out of Workington. However, the timings still permitted operation by one engine – and maybe one train crew, bearing in mind the long working hours of those days on a rural railway. The Sunday service had been reduced by this time to two trains each way. Fares had risen to 1s 8d, 1s 2d and 8½d for 1st, 2nd and 3rd Classes respectively.

By 1855 there were five advertised trips in each direction, with two trips on Sundays. In January 1855 the working day extended from the 7.20am from Cockermouth to the final arrival back at 9.15pm. By August the day was curtailed to 8.00am-9.15pm.

In 1856 it was remarked deprecatingly at a Board meeting that the company's carriage accommodation was insufficient and 'the practice of carrying passengers in trucks is dangerous'. It was not stated whether this referred to passengers riding on the goods train, or to the reinforcing of passenger trains by the attachment of goods vehicles. However, the company's stock remained at eight carriages (two 1st, two 2nd and four 3rd Class vehicles, all four-wheeled) through to 1864; in that year £375 was spent on a new (replacement?) carriage from builders Brown Marshall & Company. In 1865 the same company secured an order, at £379 10s 0d, for a composite carriage with two central 1st Class compartments and a 2nd Class compartment at each end.

From 25 August 1857 the service was reduced, but the January 1860 timetable shows overall times of operation from 7.00am ex-Cockermouth until 9.35pm at night, with five trains each way. The situation was much the same in August 1860, apart from returning 1 hour earlier with the last train from Workington to Cockermouth, arriving at 8.30pm, with three trains on Sundays.

The C&WR operated a through engine working to Whitehaven as early as 1852. Commencing in the spring of 1858, a Whitehaven Junction Railway engine and carriages ran through to Cockermouth from Whitehaven at 8.15am, returning at 9.50am from Cockermouth to Whitehaven. A balancing working at this time took the C&WR engine and carriages through at 3.30pm from Cockermouth to Whitehaven, returning at 4.30pm ex-Whitehaven, for Cockermouth. There was an alteration to the morning working from about January 1861. The Whitehaven Junction Railway's 'heavy engine' came off the train at Workington and was then otherwise employed, while the C&WR provided engine power to take the train forward at 8.51am from Workington to

A sylvan setting near Keswick, in May 1936, with a 'Cauliflower' 0-6-0 on an up passenger train. *Locomotive & General Railway Photographs*

Cockermouth and bring it back at 10.00am from Cockermouth to Workington. In the afternoon the C&WR henceforward provided motive power for the 3.05pm Workington-Whitehaven and 4.35pm return trip, the Whitehaven Junction company paying the C&WR. Presumably, the Junction company's heavy engine was more profitably employed on duties around the Workington yards and harbour.

Workington Bridge station had opened in the early years of the C&WR, being nearer to the town centre than the 'Joint station' at the site known today. Broughton developed to be 'Broughton Cross for Greysouthen'.

The C&WR's revenue from passenger operations was static at around £2,400 a year in the period 1856-58, about ten years after the opening of the line. It crept up during the years 1860-63 to reach just over £3,000 in the last year. In 1865, the last independent year of the company, it approached £4,000. Single and day return tickets, including through bookings between Whitehaven or Maryport and Cockermouth, came in during the mid-1850s. Season tickets were issued somewhat informally to individuals, but in August 1856 standard rates were fixed:

	12 months	6 months	3 months
1st Class	£8 10s 0d	£4 10s 0d	£2 10s 0d
2nd Class	£6 8s 0d	£3 5s 0d	£1 15s 0d

In June 1859, monthly tickets were introduced, at 21 shillings (1st Class) and 17 shillings (2nd). This probably contributed to the improved figures from 1860.

Comment follows on the C&WR services of 1865 and 1866, as in those years there emerged elements of co-ordination with the new CKPR – through the junction at Cockermouth and the use of a new joint passenger station in that town. A consequence of the passenger link to Penrith (effective from January 1865) was the appearance of LNWR coaching stock. In February 1866 the LNWR complained that the C&WR 'is using LNWR carriages and keeping their own stock in the shed'. The Secretary of the little C&WR was able to respond with a courteous reminder that he had agreed some time previously with Mr William Cawkwell, General Manager at Euston, to consider each company's stock as one. He pointed out that both LNWR and C&WR carriages were currently running between Workington and Penrith.

C&WR/CKPR passenger trains, 1865-1889

In preparation for the opening of the CKPR line, representatives of the LNWR, NER and CKPR met at Penrith on 17 June 1864 and drafted a passenger timetable, but in the event Euston curtailed the proposed service. This commenced on 2 January 1865 and first appeared in the February 1865 issue of 'Bradshaw,' with three trains each way:

Cockermouth: depart for Keswick and Penrith 7.00am, 11.40am and 6.40pm
Penrith: depart for Keswick and Cockermouth 9.40am, 1.45pm, 5.40pm

This fortunate picture catches an 0-4-2 tender locomotive of the Maryport & Carlisle Railway, carrying that company's number (presumably 2, 4, 15 or 16, these engines being built between 1879 and 1895 at Maryport). The train comprises two LNWR turn-of-the-century corridor coaches. There is a distinctive Bouch-designed accommodation bridge over the cutting, of a type that obtained its strength from arched lattice side girders, discussed in Chapter 3. It is probably bridge No 27 (Beck Wythop) and the train is running along the shore of Bassenthwaite on its way from Keswick to Brigham and Carlisle. The date could well be 1923-24. *Peter W. Robinson collection*

All trains were timed at 1hr 35min, with intermediate calls at Embleton, Bassenthwaite Lake, Braithwaite, Keswick, Threlkeld, Troutbeck, Penruddock and Blencowe – there were no Sunday trains. Locomotives and carriages were provided by the LNWR but, surprisingly, the service was not planned to permit its working by a single locomotive and train. On the other hand, the still-independent C&WR successfully ran an economical and self-contained service of five trains each way between Cockermouth and Workington (two each way on Sundays). However, although this company by now used the Joint upper passenger station in Cockermouth, little effort was made to ensure that trains connected there.

The CKPR 'tourist' service of that first year (1865) ran from May to October, providing in the July-August period four trains each way between Cockermouth and Penrith, accompanied by 'short' workings at 9.10am (Cockermouth-Keswick) and 10.10am (Keswick-Cockermouth). The C&WR ran six trains each way that summer, of which three in each direction made connections with the CKPR. There were two trains on Sundays over both railways. The newer spelling of 'Blencow' was adopted henceforward.

Throughout its long career (1845-1922) the LNWR boasted a hard-headed management style at Euston. The Chairman and General Manager gave their district

officers considerable scope for initiative – but this did not extend to the incurring of capital expenditure, nor to fixing the level of train services. On the CKPR their aim was to operate the most economical winter service that could be reconciled with their contractual obligation to the Keswick company. In summer they sought to create new traffic through the provision of a cautiously superior service, backed by 'tourist' fares designed to induce long-range travel to and from Lakeland. A careful watch was kept at Euston on the response to their summertime efforts. In 1866 they declined to commence the summer schedules until June, but continued them until late October. Again, in 1867, they declined the Keswick Board's request for summer services in May; the true summer workings being from July to October that year. By autumn 1868 Euston was seeking to end the seasonal service before the end of October. However, the merger of the Whitehaven Junction Railway and the Cockermouth & Workington Railway into the LNWR (by Act of 16 July 1866) led to a single integrated timetable between Whitehaven, Workington, Cockermouth, Keswick and Penrith from January 1867.

From Workington there were six trains to Cockermouth, two of which continued to Penrith, as a part of the CKPR basic service of three weekday trains. In the down direction

CKPR departures from Penrith were, on weekdays, at 8.52am, 1.45pm and 5.40pm – all running through to the coast. These three were thus part of the pattern of seven down trains provided by the LNWR from Cockermouth to Workington. The CKPR had one train each way on Sundays while the LNWR (C&WR line) ran three each way. In general, there was through running from and to Whitehaven. On the C&WR line, Marron Junction had appeared as an intermediate station from about mid-1866.

Mails

The C&WR carried mails by selected passenger trains and the LNWR inherited this traffic between Workington and Cockermouth. The CKPR looked to Post Office traffic as a potential source of revenue and by December 1866 Mr Cattle (Company Secretary) was negotiating for the carriage of mails between Penrith and Keswick, also to Cockermouth. He had at least £600 of annual revenue in mind. However, the PO seems to have been in no hurry to provide Keswick with mails by train, although with effect from 18 July 1869 they were sending mail from Carlisle to Cockermouth by Bullgill and the M&CR Derwent branch line, which had opened on 1 June 1867. Presumably at that stage delivery to Keswick would be by horse 'gig' from Cockermouth station.

At last, in August 1870, the CKPR secured a contract for mails, worth £225 a year: the Postmaster General had clearly driven a hard bargain. Keswick morning mails were now to arrive by train from Penrith. By November 1872 the PO was suggesting that the 7.15am 'Day Mail' from London Euston to Carlisle should call at Penrith at about 2.30pm, with the CKPR adjusting the time of its early afternoon train to provide a connection.

Back to basics

There were periodic slight improvements, curtailments and adjustments, but in January 1875 the service was much as it had been in January 1867; only two of the up CKPR trains came through from West Cumberland to Penrith, but all three down CKPR trains ran through from Penrith to Whitehaven.

Correspondence of October-November 1875 with the redoubtable G. P. Neele, by then Superintendent of the Line at Euston, brought a reminder that the inter-company agreement was for three trains daily in winter, but commencing during that winter this was increased to four, with the CKPR subsidising one working each way. A fifth down passenger service was achieved with minimum fuss by attaching carriages to the early morning goods train from Penrith to Cockermouth, thereby providing a 'mixed' service.

In 1877-78 a passenger carriage was also attached to the last up goods from Cockermouth, as far as Keswick; George Findlay (Traffic Manager at Euston) had initially demurred, only agreeing in return for an indemnity against all resultant liabilities. Further representations, early in 1880, led to this 'mixed' operation being extended throughout from Cockermouth to Keswick and Penrith, on the 6.20pm goods. In the same period it was arranged to attach a carriage to the afternoon goods, as between Keswick and Penrith, when required by Directors homeward bound to Penrith or beyond after CKPR Board meetings. This facility commenced about January 1878.

Beginning with the winter service of 1881-82, a note was inserted in timetables reminding that that these first down and last up advertised trains were goods trains with passenger carriages attached and 'not guaranteed'; also that passengers would travel by them 'at own risk'. From June 1882 the LNWR (principally George Findlay, by now General Manager, and G. P. Neele) secured an increased subsidy of 1s 6d per mile for one train each way between Penrith and Cockermouth during June, which was regarded as a 'marginal' month. Incidentally, winter services had settled down to commence in November each year.

Twenty years after the opening of the CKPR, the winter timetable of January 1885 was as shown in the accompanying table. This consolidated the improvements described, providing five services each way on the CKPR portion of the route. One notes that the early up train came through from West Cumberland. The 6.30am down train was

CKPR winter passenger timetable, January 1885

		am	am	am	am	pm	pm	pm	pm
WORKINGTON	(dep)	6.25 (MO)	8.15	8.30	10.52	3.08	5.40	8.24	9.40
COCKERMOUTH	(arr)	6.48 (MO)	8.45	9.00	11.19	3.38	6.10	8.52	10.8
	(dep)	6.55		9.10	11.22	3.40	6.15		
KESWICK	(dep)	7.30		9.45	11.55	4.12	6.55		
PENRITH	(arr)	8.20		10.35	12.45pm	5.00	8.00		
PENRITH	(dep)	6.30		9.55			1.40	5.30	7.20
KESWICK		7.45		10.43			2.30	6.15	8.10
COCKERMOUTH	(arr)	8.19		11.13			3.00	6.42	8.40
	(dep)	8.48	10.15	11.14	1.55pm (MO)		3.05	6.45	8.45
WORKINGTON	(arr)	9.11	10.42	11.41	2.23pm (MO)		3.33	7.13	9.13

specifically shown as 'mixed' from Penrith to Cockermouth, and the last up train would be mixed between Cockermouth (6.15pm) and Penrith (8.00pm). A 10.34am Rowrah-Cockermouth passenger service, together with Sunday trains (one of which ran each way on the CKPR) completed the service.

Summer services

Prior to 1886 the summer services were only marginally more generous than those provided in the winter of 1884-85 (mentioned above). Thus, in July 1875, five up trains were shown from Cockermouth, at 7.10am, 9.10am, 11.45am, 4.00pm and 6.25pm, all except the first running through from Whitehaven. In the down direction departures from Penrith were at 7.45am, 9.55am, 1.30pm, 2.30pm and 7.00pm – again, five advertised, all running to Workington, indeed four through to Whitehaven.

By summer 1877 two significant changes had emerged: the 5.30am 'mixed' from Penrith to Cockermouth (with connecting passenger service to Whitehaven) was acknowledged as such, while the 2.30pm ex-Penrith had been retimed to leave, probably more helpfully, at 5.10pm. By summer 1885 the 5.30am down admitted to being 'mixed', the 5.10pm down service ran at 5.45pm, and the 7.00pm down at 7.20pm.

The coming of through carriages, 1886

During the 1870s the CKPR Board received complaints about delays and other problems involved in changing trains at Penrith. Eventually, in August 1879, the Directors asked the LNWR to operate through passenger carriages, also a luggage van, for the carriage of holidaymakers' heavy trunks, cumbersome hat boxes, and other bulky possessions. They suggested running through vehicles on the 10.00am train from Euston, for the CKPR to convey to Keswick and Cockermouth, with a balancing working by the midday connection, for London. The LNWR response was to provide a better southbound connection with effect from 1 July 1880; the 12.55pm from Carlisle (1.25pm from Penrith), seemingly an up train for Manchester and Liverpool, would be extended to London, with arrival due at 8.30pm. George Findlay wrote to say that his Board did not wish to provide through carriages to and from the CKPR.

Other improved *connections* were, however, introduced about this time. From 1 June 1880 a daily summer service of trains was run between the MR's station at Appleby and Penrith, using the NER's Eden Valley route and timed to connect with the CKPR trains. The Keswick company had been seeking through bookings between its line and the MR by this link, and presumably the bookings were introduced at this time. The LNWR also provided additional trains from Penrith to Carlisle in the mid-morning period, with a return working towards 5.00pm, timed in conjunction with convenient CKPR trains.

More discussion followed. The CKPR asked the NER and the MR about through carriages, and Manager Peter Thompson met G. P. Neele (around July 1880), when the LNWR Superintendent expressed himself in favour of through vehicles. However, he shortly retracted, doubtless overruled either by his General Manager or the LNWR Board. Pressure was maintained by the determined CKPR Board and at last, in March 1886, came inklings that the LNWR proposed changes in the passenger service from 1 June.

The timetable for the period July-September 1886 included extra trains, 9.20am Penrith-Keswick and 11.00am Keswick-Penrith. The CKPR had won the argument, at least for a trial period, for the 11.00am from Keswick was actually a through train to Euston, due to arrive in the capital about 7.00pm, 'to run as an experiment during those months, at an extra payment to the LNWR of 6d per mile'. In the corresponding months of 1887, the LNWR ran a 9.18am Penrith-Keswick service (described as 'short train') and an 11.00am Keswick-Euston ('an express'). Between July and September 1888 additional trains comprised the 9.18am Penrith-Keswick and 12.50pm Keswick-Penrith, while the 11.20am ex-Cockermouth was run as a through express, between Keswick and Euston, where it was booked to arrive at 8.00pm; presumably the through carriages were attached at Keswick. Once again, the CKPR paid 6d per mile extra.

The through carriages officially advertised from Keswick during the high summer months of 1886-88 were in the up direction (to Euston) and in the last of these years (1888) were seemingly associated with a service (also with through carriages from Keswick?) due to arrive at Manchester Exchange (via Hindley Curve) at 3.40pm. The corresponding down main-line timetables show an express leaving Euston at 10.30am (1886 and 1887) and 10.40am (1888) and nominally terminating at

Penrith at 5.40pm, 5.45pm and 5.35pm, in the successive years. Departure for Keswick and the CKPR line was 10-15 minutes later – thus hinting strongly at through down workings.

In 1888 the same down main-line service gave excellent times from, alternatively, Manchester Exchange (2.25pm) and Manchester Victoria (2.35pm); it is thus possible that both up and down through carriages connected Keswick with Manchester in the summer of 1888.

Encouraged by these developments, in early 1889 the CKPR Board proposed a revision of their original 1864 working agreement with the LNWR, in order to develop traffic. The original agreement called for payment of 33⅓% of coaching receipts, in return for which the LNWR provided a basic service of three trains each way daily. The Keswick company now proposed to pay 35% – but to fix the number of trains operated. The resulting new agreement (31 January 1889) provided for 35% payment (and not less than 1 shilling per train mile for goods and passenger trains combined) but with 'the number limited as before *but by mutual agreement*'. Presumably this drafting was intentionally vague.

Thus, after 25 years of working experience, the pattern of summertime operation on the Keswick road was taking a rather more evolutionary and enterprising shape.

CKPR passenger trains, 1890-1922

The winter service of January 1885 has already been outlined. The basic pattern of five trains each way over the CKPR during 'out of season' months continued for some 15 further years. During the 1890s the last down train's departure time from Penrith was helpfully put back by about an hour – to around 8.25pm. From the early 1900s there was also a strengthening of the basic service to six trains each way. This continued until 1917-18, when wartime stringencies forced a reduction of the service to five trains in each direction, further reduced to four trains each way from April 1918.

Around this time 'colliers trains' were running, departing at 5.00am from Workington to William Pit Siding and

Summer services, 1892

Station					Express	SO						Thu SO[1]
WORKINGTON	(dep)	6.42am	8.27am	9.12am	10.41am	11.51am	1.35pm	2.55pm		5.30pm		
COCKERMOUTH	(arr)	7.01am	8.55am	9.29am	11.08am	12.08pm	2.00pm	3.22pm		5.58pm	7.10pm	8.15pm
COCKERMOUTH	(dep)	7.02am		9.30am	11.10am	12.10pm	2.08pm	3.25pm		6.00pm		
KESWICK		7.30am	10.00am[2]		11.40am	12.35pm[2]	2.55pm	3.55pm	4.50pm[1]	6.30pm		
PENRITH	(arr)	8.20am	10.45am		12.30pm	1.15pm		4.45pm	5.33pm		7.57pm	8.57pm

Station		SX	SO
WORKINGTON	(dep)	8.07pm	10.12pm
COCKERMOUTH	(arr)	8.33pm	10.40pm

Station				Thu SO[1]	MO		SO	Express[3]			
PENRITH	(dep)	7.30am	9.20am	1.15pm		1.55pm	2.50pm	5.45pm	6.20pm		8.25pm
KESWICK	(arr)	8.15am	10.00am	2.00pm		2.40pm	3.35pm	5.55pm	6.25pm	7.10pm	9.10pm
COCKERMOUTH	(arr)	8.45am	10.33am	2.32pm				6.25pm	6.55pm	7.43pm	9.42pm
COCKERMOUTH	(dep)	8.48am	10.34am	2.34pm	1.50pm			6.27pm	6.57pm	7.46pm	9.45pm
WORKINGTON	(arr)	9.13am	10.58am	2.59pm	2.17pm			6.49pm	7.19pm	8.12pm	10.02pm

[1] Indicates through trains between Keswick and Carlisle or vice versa.

[2] Through carriages left Keswick at 10.00am for Euston (due 6.10pm) and for Manchester Exchange (due 2.00pm); also Keswick 12.35pm for Euston (due 8.40pm).

[3] The first portion (from Preston) of the 10.40am Euston-Carlisle conveyed through carriages from Euston to Keswick, also from Manchester Exchange (dep 2.30pm) to Keswick – the Keswick vehicles from both London and Manchester were attached to the 5.45pm express over the CKPR, from Penrith.

Most trains shown above from and to Workington came through from, or ran to, Whitehaven at this period.
There was a passenger train into Cockermouth at 8.40am (MO), which came from Whitehaven via Moor Row, Rowrah and the direct eastern curve at Marron Junction. Return was at 3.30pm (MO) from Cockermouth to Rowrah.
On the CKPR, there were two trains each way on Sundays.

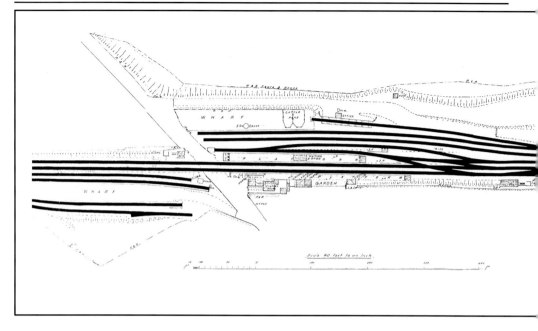

Brigham level crossing and station are shown on this LMS plan, with two signal boxes still in use: No 1 is to the east (opposite the junction) and No 2 is westerly, by the level crossing. Note the M&CR back platform road and loop, on the north side of the passenger station, and the M&CR Derwent branch to Bullgill, with the bridge that collapsed on 16 December 1936.

leaving there for Workington at 5.50am. There was also a 1.05pm SX Workington-William Pit Siding (SO it ran as the 1.05pm Workington-Cockermouth passenger). 'Workmen's trains' were the 8.55pm Workington-Cockermouth and 9.40pm Cockermouth-Workington, and on Sundays the 5.15am Cockermouth-Workington and 5.35am Workington-Cockermouth passenger. Keswick offered a quarry workers' train at 7.05am to Threlkeld, with a return working from Threlkeld at 5.40pm SX (12.45pm SO).

The M&CR ran several daily passenger services between Cockermouth via Brigham (reverse) and the Derwent Branch, thence to Bullgill. West of Cockermouth, it is interesting to note three trains daily from Whitehaven to Workington by 'the long way round' via Cleator Moor, the Joint Line and Marron Junction (taking 1hr 15min to 1hr 21min). Southbound over the Joint Line there were two trains: the 7.50am ex-Workington, and

the interesting 3.20pm ex-Cockermouth, which reversed at Marron Junction (3.33-3.38pm). By this time, the direct east-south chord at Marron had been severed.

A basic six trains (each way) were reinstated after the war and this was the pattern in both1921 and 1922, as the CKPR's days of 'independence' ran out. No evidence has been found of 'mixed' trains in the period from the 1890s onward.

The M&CR showed modest enterprise in the period discussed. Its Derwent Branch from Bullgill to Brigham, which linked the M&CR main line with the C&WR, had been opened during 1867 (just after the C&WR became part of the LNWR), and from 1 November 1867 they were to run to Cockermouth passenger station, exercising running powers under an agreement with the LNWR and CKPR, concluded at Euston on 17 October 1867. They duly ran passenger trains (which reversed at Brigham) to Cockermouth on weekdays. In the spring of 1920 the company arranged to run a Sunday train from Carlisle to Cockermouth and return, with its own engine and carriages. The M&CR wished to run forward to Keswick on Sundays, but the LNWR declined either to permit this, or to do it themselves. On weekdays from 1919 the

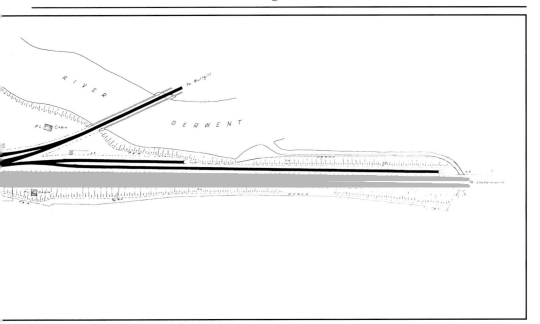

M&CR had been allowed to run empty stock between Cockermouth and Keswick in order to form a 9.45am passenger service from Keswick to Cockermouth and the M&CR line.

By November 1920 the M&CR engine and carriage was enabled to convey passengers into Keswick (at 8.48am) and out again, the jealous guardians of the CKPR (at Euston) justifying their 'concession' as a help to children from Cockermouth travelling to Keswick School. The single to-and-fro working continued during 1921-22, and by spring 1922 had been joined by a 'teatime' working, due into Keswick at 6.05pm and out again at 6.30pm, to the M&CR. Cecil J. Allen (in *The Railway Magazine* of 1921) recorded the 9.45am ex-Keswick as comprising a single LNWR corridor composite coach, lettered 'on loan to Maryport and Carlisle Railway' and running through to Carlisle all year round. Its locomotive was provided by the M&CR.

Summer services
Summer services (primarily July-September) continued to produce interesting changes and improvements during the period 1890-1914. The version for 1892 is shown in the table on page 25.

During the 1890s the summer pattern of passenger services on the line continued to provide five up passenger trains daily over the full length of the CKPR, as well as one up service from the west, terminating at Keswick. Two trains started from Keswick to proceed eastward. In addition there were six down services from Penrith over the CKPR, plus one other that ran from Penrith to Keswick. In simple terms the service could be summarised as providing 6½ trains each way!

From 1900 the CKPR service was developed to seven trains each way in summer. An extra working in and out of Keswick from/to Workington raised the figure to 7½ each way from 1903. From January 1904, by agreement with LNWR Superintendent of the Line Robert Turnbull, day return tickets were issued on one day weekly from Cockermouth (11 shillings) and Keswick (10 shillings) to Liverpool and Manchester in order to encourage out-and-back travel. There were also tentative experiments with residential travel, which had been a successful feature of the Windermere line since 1875. An experiment in summer 1902 with a Keswick-Manchester (and Liverpool) train (departing at about 7.15am MO) was, however, a dismal failure, and in May 1906 Mr

Turnbull told the CKPR Board that there was no thought of repeating it – although, in 1910-11, a 7.10am MO Keswick-Oxenholme was tried, connecting with the Windermere-Manchester residential train.

Summer 1906 witnessed further improvement. In the up direction there was an additional train at 8.30am (ex-Workington) due into Penrith 10.25am, but no 'short' workings on the CKPR proper; thus there were eight up trains. In the down direction there were seven through trains, with a further train running only as far as Keswick, and another that started there. Thus effectively there were eight down services. The summers of 1907-09 were served very similarly.

During the summers of 1910-14 the level of service was the equivalent of nine up and '8½' down, eight trains each way actually running over the whole of the CKPR, the remainder representing workings on the eastern (Keswick-Penrith) portion of the line only.

There were some Keswick-Penrith-Carlisle through workings. However, the long-range through carriages were mainly between Keswick and Euston (tending, as time passed, to run from Whitehaven or Workington, via Keswick, to Euston, and return). In 1898 they were seemingly included in the 9.45am up train from Keswick (arrive Euston 6.00pm) and the 1.30pm up service (arrive Euston 9.20pm). The first of these services, on the LNWR main line, was styled the 'Keswick and Windermere Express', while the second was titled 'Lakes Express', a name that became very familiar indeed much later. The same year through carriages ran to Keswick in the 10.25am departure from Euston, a train grandly known as the 'Cambrian, Central Wales and English Lakes Express'; departure was at 5.03pm from Penrith, due into Keswick at 5.50pm. It is not clear whether Manchester-Keswick through carriages were run at this time.

By 1905 the London carriages were included in the 9.00am up train from Keswick. In 1906 the favoured train was the 9.00am up service (arrive Euston 5.05pm) and probably also the 11.45am up duty (attached to the up Perth train, due at Euston at 7.10pm). In the down direction in 1906 a 10.10am ex-Euston train served Morecambe, the Furness line, Windermere and Keswick; there was a non-stop run from Stafford to Lancaster calling at Penrith (5.04pm-5.10pm, involving reversal), reaching Keswick at 5.55pm.

From Manchester Exchange the first portion of a 3.03pm departure reached Penrith at 5.37pm and clearly proceeded as the 5.45pm express over the CKPR line, due to arrive at Keswick at 6.28pm. In 1907 the 3.03pm from Manchester Exchange ran to Morecambe, also to the FR line, and not apparently to Keswick. At that time Keswick had Euston carriages in the 9.00am and 1.45pm up trains, and also had two down services from Euston – at 10.10am (arrive Keswick 5.55pm, as in the previous year) and 11.30am (second portion from Preston, off a Scots express, reaching Keswick at 6.35pm). The same two up through services operated in 1908, leaving Keswick at 9.00am and 1.45pm, and the through vehicles probably came down with the 10.10am and in rear of the 11.30am Scots train, being included in the CKPR's 5.10pm and 5.45pm trains respectively (from Penrith). In 1909 the two up workings ran in the same paths. In the down direction the through carriages were clearly included in the 5.10pm from Penrith, less clearly in the 5.45pm.

It was the expansion of through carriage workings that stepped up the summer service from 1910. In that year Keswick enjoyed the services of up through carriages to Euston (two services), Manchester Exchange, Manchester Victoria and Liverpool Exchange. Vehicles for Euston were attached at Keswick at 9.00am, for arrival in London at 5.05pm as part of the up 'Keswick and Windermere Express'. The 1.45pm working at Keswick (12.20pm ex-Whitehaven) conveyed through carriages from Keswick for attachment at Penrith to the 12 noon Glasgow/Edinburgh-Euston, due 8.30pm. In addition to the Keswick-Euston 57-foot Brake Tri-composite carriage, there were two vehicles for Manchester Exchange and one for Manchester Victoria; these three were detached at Preston from the same main-line express. A 6.05pm departure from Keswick was run to take a through carriage for Liverpool Exchange, which formed part of the 4.30pm Glasgow-Manchester/Liverpool express as between Penrith and Preston.

In the down direction the 10.10am Euston-Blackpool and the Lakes conveyed a carriage from London to Keswick and (from Stafford north) through vehicles from Birmingham to Keswick. The 11.30am down service for Scotland included two carriages for Keswick, coming off at Preston and going north with through carriages for Keswick from the 2.35pm ex-Manchester Victoria and 2.52pm ex-Liverpool Exchange (as well as London Euston/Manchester Exchange-Windermere through vehicles, to be left behind at Oxenholme). At this time a move was apparent to develop 'day return' traffic inwards to the Keswick line, as witnessed by an arrival from the south at Penrith at 9.07am, with a 9.30am Penrith-CKPR line train in connection. The 6.05pm train, originating at Keswick and calling only at Troutbeck en route to Penrith, connected into the evening Glasgow-Manchester/Liverpool, and (as explained above) two vehicles ran through from Keswick to Liverpool. It is not too clear whether the Liverpool through carriages continued as such in later years, but in 1914 the 6.05pm train was specifically advertised as running from Keswick to Preston.

The North Eastern Railway
The NER had been prominent in the development of day excursion trips to Keswick via Stainmore, the Eden Valley line and the Eamont-Redhills NER link, with very early starts from Hull, York or Durham colliery districts. An intriguing item in the history of NER coaching stock was its vehicle No 104, built in 1896. It was a bogie lavatory Composite with four 1st Class and two 3rd Class compartments, on record as being intended for a King's Cross and Penrith service. If this ever ran, it would surely be operated primarily in summer and extended to Keswick. There was a companion vehicle, perhaps intended for a balancing working.

A daily Darlington-Keswick train service ran first, it is believed, in the summer of 1906 and could account for the 11.05am Penrith-Keswick (terminating 11.43am), introduced that year. During following years the 11.43am ex-Penrith ran through to Whitehaven. In the summers between 1911 and 1914 through carriages operated from York and Newcastle-upon-Tyne, both via Stainmore to/from Keswick, and would be designed to encourage period ('tourist') return travel.

The Midland Railway
The Midland Railway came into the picture too. From the summer of 1910 – and likewise in 1911 and 1912 – there were through carriages from Leeds to Keswick, in the 10.00am Leeds Midland-Glasgow St Enoch train, which was purposely diverted to run via Ingleton and Penrith. The through vehicles used the new 12.15pm Penrith-Keswick train, terminating at 12.50pm, which was indeed a conveniently timed tourist service. The new up express on the CKPR started from Keswick at 12.35pm and included Keswick-Leeds coaches for transfer at Penrith to the 10.30am Edinburgh Waverley-Leeds-St Pancras train, routed via Ingleton. During 1913 and 1914 the MR service in question was somewhat curtailed; it ran four days weekly in high summer (Monday, Tuesday, Friday and Saturday), at 9.35am from Leeds. The up working remained around midday – in July 1914 the express started from Keswick at 12.35pm for Leeds.

The CKPR favoured restoration of the Leeds-Keswick through workings after the war years, but in summer 1920 the LNWR and MR combined to refuse the facility. Note, however, that a Leeds-Keswick summer service was run, via Carnforth, and (in the LMS period) it ran each summer from 1923 to 1926 (inclusive) via the Ingleton route, at first on four days weekly but later on Saturdays only. And there was a revival during the peak period of the summers of 1922-39 (inclusive) on FSO, subsequently moving to SO.

The 1914 peak
In the summer of 1914 booked through workings from Keswick reached their peak:

1 7.10am MO Keswick-Oxenholme, which connected into the Windermere-Manchester

'club' residential train and was aimed at businessmen, who might join their families for the weekend before returning to town on Monday morning.

2 8.30am from Workington (9.00am from Cockermouth, 9.38am from Keswick), which ran through to Euston (arrive 5.07pm).

3 8.15am from Whitehaven (9.15 from Cockermouth, 9.52am from Keswick), which included through carriages to Carlisle (arrive 11.20am).

4 12.35pm (Monday, Tuesday, Friday, Saturday) from Keswick, the through express (via Ingleton) to Leeds (arrive 4.10pm).

5 12.20pm from Whitehaven (1.45pm from Keswick), which may well have conveyed through carriages into the 12 noon Glasgow/Edinburgh-Euston (8.30pm), and for Manchester too.

6 2.47pm from Workington (3.55pm from Keswick), a through train to Carlisle (arrive 5.07pm).

7 6.10pm from Keswick, a through train to Preston.

A down working at 6.45am (MSO) from Manchester Victoria in that summer was seemingly run through to Keswick, where it was booked to arrive at 11.00am. Certainly the 2.55pm from Manchester Exchange (due to arrive at Keswick at 6.28pm and Whitehaven at 7.58pm) was a through train, with a portion for Windermere, detached en route. There was also the 9.35am service from Leeds (Monday, Tuesday, Friday, Saturday) to Keswick. The down Euston through service is a little obscure, but Bletchley originated a through carriage at 11.03am for Keswick, leaving Penrith at 5.10pm and reaching its destination at 5.55pm. A portion from Birmingham was probably included in the same main-line train. The 5.45pm from Penrith conveyed a Carlisle-Workington carriage.

Wartime summers, 1914-18

The wartime summer service on the Keswick road was reduced by 1917 to the five passenger trains operated each way over the CKPR, as in corresponding winters, with no 'short' or long-range passenger workings anywhere between Penrith and Cockermouth. The Cockermouth-Workington line of the LNWR only benefited from the same five trains, accompanied by the all-year 7.40am train from Cockermouth-Workington and 1.05pm SO Workington-Cockermouth, both intended for such folk as shop-workers. There were also the workmen's and colliers' trains and the all-year trains to and from the Joint Line, and five M&CR trains each way to and from Cockermouth, with extra services on Monday for the market traffic. From 1 April 1918 a further 'squeeze' was apparent.

Latter-day summers on the CKPR, 1919-22

In the spring of 1919 there were slight improvements, and during that summer the basic service on the CKPR reverted to six trains each way. In addition a 10.00am Keswick-Euston through train appeared (to run until the end of September), combining with a Windermere portion and restaurant car at Oxenholme. Down through carriages for Keswick were provided in the 11.15am Euston-Windermere train, these being worked to Penrith and run in the 6.25pm daily CKPR train, from which they were detached at Keswick at 7.08pm.

There was no basic change by the summer of 1921, but the through carriages were run from both Workington and Keswick, at 9.15am from Workington (Cockermouth at 9.35am, Keswick 10.10am), so providing a seventh up train throughout – and they reached Euston at 6.05pm. These coaches probably came down in the 10.40am train from Euston and were attached to the 6.00pm departure from Penrith to Workington. There were still no booked Sunday trains at this time, even in summer.

LMS era passenger trains, 1923-1945

The basic service continued at six trains each way (as in much of the 1904-22 period)

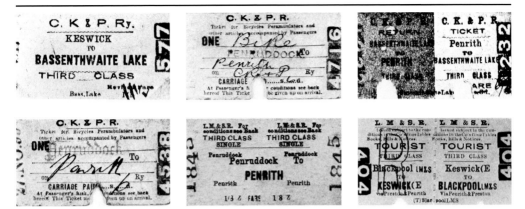

A selection of tickets, illustrating some of the styles employed. The bicycle tickets of 1899 and 1907 were white. The LMS tickets shown are green; the one from Penruddock is dated 17 NO 49 and the 'Tourist' ticket is from early days of the LMS, as witness the style of the serial numbers (as used also on the CKPR). *Courtesy of C. C. Green, G. Lord, Denis R. Perriam and Mrs M. Ridley*

through to 1939. Their departure times from Cockermouth (up) and Penrith (down) continued to vary a little from year to year but, in general, remained incredibly close to those applying early in the 20th century.

A 'short' working worthy of comment was derived from M&CR practice of 1920; it ran into Cockermouth from the west and through to Keswick, where it arrived at 8.47am. Departure was at 10.00am. It then returned at 6.08pm, leaving again at 6.30pm. With variants in some years, these workings conveyed a through carriage from Carlisle (via Bullgill) and Brigham (reverse). This obviously provided a valuable link between Cockermouth and Carlisle. One might doubt whether the same would be true round the western end of the Skiddaw mountain barrier.

It is revealing to see the value of this service, even from Keswick to Carlisle and back, demonstrated on a typical weekday in 1934, when the outward journey by the 'conventional' route via Penrith and the WCML departed Keswick at 9.39am, due at Carlisle at 11.35am, with 50 minutes to wait at Penrith. The alternative was to depart Keswick at 9.56am and arrive at Carlisle at 11.43am via Brigham, snug in a through carriage! Returning, the WCML departure was from Carlisle at 4.35pm, due at Keswick at 7.00pm – with 64 minutes wait at Penrith, as against leaving Carlisle at 4.20pm and

arriving at Keswick at 6.09pm, again in the through carriage via Brigham.

In each case the overall time between Keswick and Carlisle much exceeded that taken by a motor car of 1934 on the roads of that day, but the through carriage by the former M&CR's Brigham route was a comfortable corridor coach 'cascaded' (in present-day parlance) from former main-line duties and the times were not unreasonable. The poor link provided at Penrith in each direction reflects not only the problems of connecting with both up and down main-line trains, but also the prevailing disregard for the economics of secondary routes such as the CKPR.

The former M&CR Brigham-Bullgill line closed entirely from 29 April 1935; a morning school-time train into Keswick from the west and out again, as well as a late afternoon trip in and out, were run for a few years at times akin to the 'M&CR trips', but they were from/to Workington and did not provide Keswick with a Carlisle service.

Between 1939 and 1945 wartime again curtailed the basic services from six to five each way daily. Typically, through Workington-Penrith trains of January 1944 appeared thus on the CKPR section:

Cockermouth: depart for Penrith 7.12am, 11.27am, 2.38pm, 5.48pm and 6.43pm

LMS-built non-corridor coaching stock is headed by 'Cauliflower' No 28589, still lettered 'LMS', climbing away from the WCML at Penrith No 1 box in August 1950 – a scene typical of the 1930s-'50s period. *E. S. Russell*

With 'express lamps', a 'Cauliflower' (No 8358, of Workington shed, withdrawn in 1930) and a 'Jumbo' 2-4-0 leave the up back platform at Keswick in the later 1920s. The LNWR and early LMS-built coaching stock is painted in LMS red livery. A wagon stabled in the bay is fitted with gas containers for recharging the cylinders of gas-lit rolling-stock. *Roy Anderson collection*

The through train from Glasgow has arrived at Keswick behind 'Cauliflower' 0-6-0 No 8318 on Sunday 20 August 1939. LNER corridor stock is also prominent, likely to return to Newcastle-upon-Tyne or another NE destination during the evening. *Herbert Gelder, courtesy of Frank Alcock*

Penrith: depart for Cockermouth 7.35am, 10.07am, 1.25pm, 4.53pmSX, 6.23pmSO and 8.10pm

There were also:

8.25am Workington-Cockermouth (arrive 8.52am)
11.50am SO Workington-Keswick (arrive 12.45)

8.55pmSX (10.30amSO) Workington-Cockermouth
7.25am Cockermouth-Whitehaven
1.05pm SO Keswick-Workington
4.15pm SO Cockermouth-Workington

This represented a more enlightened spread than was provided in the depths of the First World War.

LMS era summer services

In general, summer services featured six Monday-Friday trains in each direction on the CKPR section, as well as two long-distance trains, one to/from Euston, the other to/from Manchester Victoria; in each case Workington was the western terminal point. No original Saturday extras appeared in the timetables. Taking summer 1930, this pattern of six 'local' trains each way applied, together with:

11.35am SO: Keswick-Carlisle
5.05pm: Keswick-Penrith
9.40am: Penrith-Workington semi-fast
2.13pm: Penrith-Keswick
5.43pm: • Penrith-Keswick express (with connection out of the 10.40am Euston-Carlisle)

9.05am from Workington (calling at Keswick from 9.56-10.08am) to Euston (5.20pm), styled 'The Lakes Express' and with through carriages from Workington, Keswick, Windermere and Blackpool Talbot Road to Euston (and Blackpool-Birmingham SX), the restaurant car being from Windermere

11.35am 'The Lakes Express' from Euston, conveying a portion for the CKPR line to Keswick (6.51pm) and Workington (7.42pm)

11.45am Workington (Keswick, depart 12.36pm) to Penrith express, with through carriages from Workington and Keswick to Manchester Victoria, attached at Preston to the 10.45am Glasgow-Manchester/Liverpool restaurant car express, due at Victoria at 4.27pm

9.40am Manchester Victoria to Keswick and Workington through carriages, attached between Preston and Penrith to the long-lived 9.25am Crewe-Perth service.

The end of the 1930s provided eight Monday-Friday trains over the CKPR road, but only one was a long-distance service, the 9.05am Workington-Euston (due 4.50pm), being 'The Lakes Express'. On Saturdays in July and August 1939 the 'Lakes' ran at 9.05am from Workington and 12 noon from Euston (the latter due into Keswick at 6.27pm, then through to Workington). There were also:

10.52amSO Liverpool Exchange (not Manchester) to Keswick (due 2.48pm), but with no corresponding up through working advertised

12.47pmSO Leeds City to Keswick (due at 4.53pm) routed via Ingleton

10.10amSO Keswick to Leeds City (due 2.05pm) routed via Ingleton

Incidentally, there was a history of Leeds-Keswick-Workington running back in 1923, as well as in pre-1914 years.

Sunday trains had generally been notable by their absence from the Keswick line since 15 April 1917, but a remarkable development of the later 1920s was a restaurant car express on Sundays in summer from Glasgow St Enoch (9.55am), calling at Kilmarnock, Dumfries, Annan, Carlisle and Penrith, then due at Keswick at 1.52pm. The train returned at 6.55pm from Keswick, with the same calls to St Enoch, where arrival was due at 10.46pm. The times quoted are those of 1939. This service probably originated in 1927. In August 1929 David L. Smith (the GSWR historian) travelled with nine carriages (277 tons) behind 'Compound' 4-4-0 No 1179 of Glasgow (Corkerhill) shed to Carlisle, whence an LNWR 'Cauliflower' 0-6-0 and an LNWR 'Jumbo' 2-4-0 combined to run briskly to Keswick, and later back again to Carlisle. The train was aimed principally at excursion passengers, providing out-and-back travel within the day at a 'bargain' rate. Likewise, each Sunday in summer, a Newcastle-upon-Tyne-Keswick train was operated, via Carlisle (reverse), reaching Keswick at 1.06pm and departing homeward at 7.10pm; this too was essentially a day excursion service. Sunday local trains were limited, in 1939 to one working into Keswick from the west and out again in the evening – directed at 'half-day' trippers.

The August 1944 service followed closely that already quoted for January 1944 with, additionally a 12.30pmSO Keswick-Penrith and a 3.35pmSO Workington-Cockermouth. These trains were accompanied by a single (one way only) long-range through service, namely through carriages leaving Liverpool Exchange at 8.10amSO for Keswick, completing their journey as the 11.13amSO Penrith-Keswick service, which arrived at 11.55am and terminated.

It is interesting that Liverpool now figured, privileged in place of Manchester and London. Had this some social reason, perhaps a number of Merseyside families still billeted in northern Lakeland due to earlier air attacks on Liverpool?

Last years of the LMS, 1946-48

From 7 October 1946 the LMS attempted to restore many train services and timings to something approaching their 1938-39 standards. The results were praiseworthy on principal main lines, but, sadly, 'nothing to write home about' on secondary and branch routes such as the Penrith-Workington line. The timetable of 7 October 1946, intended to operate until 4 May 1947 (but not helped by the coal shortage of 1947) showed a basic seven trains each way, accompanied by a few 'short' workings. The starting times differed considerably from the remarkably stable pattern of the 1904-39 period. No serious attempt was made to connect passengers with Carlisle, at Penrith, and there were similarly few useful southerly main-line connections. The total train mileage advertised on the Keswick line was clearly adequate for all needs, but when the train times are examined in detail one wonders who was expected to travel, as neither workers nor shoppers were neatly provided for – and not even scholars. The tale is all too typical of railway management, and not only in 1946.

By 1947-48 there was a curtailment to six trains in each direction – and still no attempt to run to or from Carlisle, nor to connect with that county town. At the west end of the route the unbalanced 7.25am Cockermouth-Workington (due 7.51am) was withdrawn mid-term, in April 1948, thus permitting no arrival in Workington before 9.18am.

BR passenger services from 1 January 1948

In the first summer of the new British Railways regime's operations (1948), the six trains each way basic service was supplemented by three up (two SO and one running three days weekly) and one down (SO). However, long-range through carriages operated, in some cases attached to basic all-year trains:

9.10am Keswick to Manchester Victoria (due 1.16pm), SO
10.20am Manchester Victoria to Keswick, SO
10.00am Workington (Keswick 11.8am) to Liverpool Exchange (due 2.35pm), SO
8.35am Workington (Keswick 9.38am) to Euston (5.25pmSX, 5.10pmSO), Mon/Fri/Sat
11.55am Euston to Workington, Mon/Fri/Sat

The coming of the diesels, 1955

Diesel multiple unit (DMU) train sets were introduced to the Keswick route from 3 January 1955, among the first examples of this innovation anywhere on BR. They soon took over the basic all-year workings, and by the spring of 1956 there were eight trains in each direction between Workington, Cockermouth, Keswick and Penrith, of which four up and three down services were through to/from Carlisle, a long-needed reform. Moreover, the journey times were much reduced. The pattern of eight DMUs each way (plus two or three longer-range steam-hauled corridor trains that ran for a summer season) became established and is seen in 1957 (17 June-15 September) and 1961 (12 June-10 September). In 1961 the basic summer departures were as follows, '(C)' indicating running to/from Carlisle:

From Cockermouth (up): 7.25am (C), 10.10am (C), 11.48am, 12.44pm (C), 1.48pm, 3.26pm, 5.49pm (C), 7.31pm (C)
From Penrith (down): 7.18am, 10.20am (C), 11.38am (C), 12.07pmSO, 1.30pm, 3.25pm, 5.00pm, 6.08pm (C), 8.32pm (C)

The 'dated' trains were:

8.20am Workington to Manchester Victoria (1.24pm)/Crewe (1.36pm), SO
10.15am Manchester Victoria to Keswick, through carriage on a Workington train, SO
8.55am* Workington to Euston (5.45pm), combining with a Windermere portion
11.35am* Euston to Workington
(*SX, with variation on SO)

Above Three LMS coaches form the up 'Lakes Express', with Ivatt Class '2MT' No 46491 at its head, as it coasts downhill towards Penrith No 1 signal box in June 1963, while Stanier 'Black 5' 4-6-0 No 45135 stands in the down loop with a mixed freight, awaiting a clear road north. The train is carrying Ford Anglia and Classic models on a pair of flat bolster wagons. *Derek Cross*

Right The large vacuum-operated turntable at Keswick dated from the summer of 1939. *David Jenkinson*

Right With the bridge strengthening complete and the new turntable in use at Keswick, by the summer of 1939 large tender engines could work the line. No 46136 *The Border Regiment*, a 'Rebuilt Scot' 4-6-0, climbs out of Penrith with 11 mixed LNER (Gresley) and BR-built coaches forming the 10.00am Newcastle-Keswick train of Sunday 1 September 1957. *Robert Leslie*

A two-car 'Derby lightweight' DMU, led by Driving Trailer Composite No M79607, leaves Penrith en route for Workington, probably in 1955 when these units were first introduced on the route. The train is painted in BR green livery, with yellow lining, and features the BR 'lion and wheel' emblem. *National Railway Museum, York*

A sunny day at Penruddock finds another two-car 'Derby lightweight' DMU leaving the up platform bound for Penrith – note the staggered platforms. By this time the livery had been modified to include a yellow warning panel between the buffer beam and the driver's windows. This followed complaints by permanent way men and other railway staff that these units were not easily visible when approaching. In later days, all-over yellow ends were standardised for all multiple units and locomotives. *David Tee*

A pleasant scene at the east end of Keswick station as a two-car 'Derby lightweight' DMU coasts into the platform en route from Penrith to Workington, probably during 1955. The replacement No 1 signal box, built by the LMS, was fitted with a Midland Railway-style lever frame at the back of the box, which meant that the signalman had to work the levers (most illogically and very inconveniently) with his back to the passing traffic. *National Railway Museum, York*

Sunday workings included Newcastle-Keswick and back, but not the Glasgow-Keswick train of 1939.

Very similar arrangements continued during the 1962-65 period inclusive, DMUs being supplemented by 'The Lakes Express' (Keswick and Workington portion) and the Manchester train. By 1964 the summer service of DMU trains was marginally expanded and the Newcastle-Keswick (and back) working on Sunday had become a DMU from 1961 and was still such in 1964.

Decline and withdrawal of services, 1966-72

When the timetable for the period 18 April 1966 to 5 March 1967 was published, it showed an all-DMU service equivalent to 6½ trains SX (5½ SO), primarily to and from Carlisle, but with no 'Lakes Express' or other long-range trains, even on summer Saturdays. A Sunday service was to run from 19 June until 4 September 1966, but with the few Sunday trains notably including the Newcastle-Keswick DMU (due in at 12.53pm) and its return working (at 18.50 from Keswick).

In the event, this half-hearted proposition was stillborn, as from 18 April 1966 the whole route west of Keswick, through Cockermouth to Derwent Junction (Workington), was closed to traffic and only a truncated service could be continued, on the eastern end of the line, namely between Keswick and Penrith, and to/from Carlisle.

The timetable from 6 March 1967

(nominally effective until 5 May 1968) acknowledged these limitations and offered a basic service of five trains each way, all but one to/from Carlisle, and six trains during the summer (mid-June to 2 September 1967), plus a seventh service coming up from Keswick on summer Saturdays. No long-range trains were advertised, nor were there any through carriage workings. The winter arrangements called for no crossings of up and down passenger trains on the CKPR line and so pointed to the pattern of 4 December 1967, from which date the double track sections, most of Keswick's surviving track layout and the signal boxes were taken out of use, leaving a single track route from Keswick to Penrith No 1 box, with only one train allowed to operate at a time. The line had become, effectively, a long siding. This extremely basic form was displayed in, for example, the timetables of 1970 (4 May)-1971 (2 May), providing six DMUs from Keswick to Penrith, of which two ran through to Carlisle, and six DMUs from Penrith to Keswick, of which two came through from Carlisle.

There were no advertised extra trains in summer and no trains on Sundays. Not surprisingly in these circumstances, the

The last day on Lakeland's northern railway. In suitably mournful conditions, a seven-car DMU rolls through the Cumberland countryside near Penruddock on 6 March 1972, providing one of the last passenger links on the truncated 'long siding' between Penrith and Keswick. *Peter W. Robinson*

service was finally abandoned before the 1971-72 timetable year was completed, with effect from 6 March 1972. So, with two-car DMUs ill-supported in winter and sometimes disgracefully overcrowded in summer, Lakeland's delightful northern railway route ended its days – apart from a little residual stone traffic at its eastern end, which itself did not long continue – and one known special working. This last train ran on Thursday 22 April 1972, when at about 5.20am a special passenger train of four vehicles was hauled by a Class 25 diesel-electric locomotive (with steam heating van attached) from Penrith No 1 box on to the branch and stabled on the gradient with all handbrakes secured and scotches placed under the carriage wheels. This was a Royal Train, which had come overnight from Euston and was thus stabled until departure at 9.45am for Carlisle, where the Princess being conveyed had duties to perform.

The actual time taken by a stopping passenger train from Penrith to Workington in the 1870s (inclusive of some 8 minutes standing time at Keswick and Cockermouth combined) was 115-118 minutes, reduced to about 110 minutes in the late 1940s. The up journey, from Workington to Penrith, occupied 121-127 minutes in the 1870s and 112 minutes in the late 1940s. Two stations, Marron and Broughton Cross (both on the Cockermouth and Workington section) had been closed in the meantime, so the figures were closely comparable, some 70 years apart. Aided by relaxation of speed restrictions over bridges, which still applied to steam-hauled trains, the introduction of DMU working effected a remarkable overall acceleration in the 1950s to (typically) 75-78 minutes, further tightened to 69-73 minutes by 1961 for down (westbound) trains and 81-86 minutes, tightened again to 79 minutes in the up (eastbound) direction. The overall time between Penrith and Workington for the steam-hauled 'Lakes Express' of summer 1961 was 93 minutes (SX) or 107 minutes (SO); there were fewer stops than in the foregoing examples of DMU timings, but considerably heavier loadings on Saturdays.

Promotion of passenger travel on the CKPR

In good time for the opening of the CKPR to passengers (effective January 1865), its representatives had met with those of the LNWR and NER (S&DR) in June-July 1864 and agreed that passengers would in general have the alternatives of 1st and 2nd Class carriages. However, there would also be 'Government class' – popularly known as 'parliamentary' – on the first and last trains daily. Through bookings were to be given for passengers, parcels, horse and carriage traffic, dogs – and goods generally – but not all stations on the three companies' lines were included in the bookings at first.

'Tourist fares' were to be available from LNWR stations south of Preston through to Keswick, with break of journey permitted at any station between Penrith and Keswick – and passengers had the option of returning by way of Windermere if they wished. This last provision implies the existence of commercial arrangements with the proprietors of coaches running from Keswick to Windermere station, via the road (now the A591) over Dunmail Raise, 'The Swan' (Grasmere) and Ambleside. The LNWR and the coach operators had probably provided a service from the south to Keswick by this route before the CKPR was promoted. The title 'circular tour tickets' was soon adopted. In 1870 the CKPR and LNWR were arranging to share the cost of the coach fare between Windermere and Keswick in agreed proportions. From 1878 Messrs Cook & Sons' 'coupon tourist tickets' were accepted, with Cooks permitted to retain 10% of the fares as commission.

After a couple of years of operation, the CKPR's Board heard in 1867 that the LNWR's District Manager had received instructions from his headquarters 'to take all the good carriages from this line and substitute inferior ones'. Remonstrances followed, pointing to the working agreement, and presumably the LNWR thought better of its plan to downrate CKPR facilities..

There was some passenger travel in goods trains and, in 1868, it was agreed to discourage this. Where this practice was allowed, passengers were to sign an indemnity form, relieving the company of responsibility, much as has applied in Scotland to recent years. Goods brake vans would provide spartan, but cosy, travel in winter. It was not so in passenger compartments, and in November 1872 the decision was taken to provide footwarmers in 1st and 2nd Class carriages.

The classes of accommodation constantly preoccupied the railway companies. In May 1872 the CKPR decided to book 3rd Class by all trains on its line, but a year later it was ruled that, as from 1 June 1873, '3rd' tickets would only be issued for the first morning train from Penrith or Cockermouth, as during an earlier period. At the same time the '2nd' single rate was reduced from 1¾d to 1½d per mile ('1st' being 2½d per mile, unchanged). At this period a government duty was still payable by railway companies on some 3rd Class fares and, in November 1874, the CKPR proposed to pass on the charge to travellers by adding 5% to the relevant fares. The Midland Railway, looking to the impending opening of its newly engineered Settle & Carlisle main line, as well as expansion of its Scottish business as a result, publicised a Board resolution of 7 October 1874 to discontinue 2nd Class carriages and reduce 1st Class fares – but at the same time abolishing return tickets at reduced fares on its system – from 1 January 1875. Incidentally, an exception to this was the Tilbury boat trains, which retained 2nd Class until much later times.

From 1 January 1878 the CKPR offered 3rd Class fares between all stations, by all trains; but this was not the end of the debate as, from the beginning of 1881, the LNWR and M&CR reduced passenger fares and the CKPR determined to adopt a new scale: 1st Class was to be 1⅝d per mile, with return at double; 2nd was 1¼d per mile, also with return at double the single fare; and 3rd was restricted to 'parliamentary' bookings (this restriction was abandoned in course of time).

Much later, from 1 January 1912, the LNWR was the leader of a group of companies that followed the MR's example of 1875 and abolished 2nd Class travel (apart from some inner London suburban services). The CKPR's Board promptly adopted the traditional stance of King Canute; the LNWR's decision had nothing to do with them and the waves could wash around them. Frank Ree, General Manager of the LNWR, had to point out (in August 1911) that all passenger trains serving the CKPR were through to or from his company's West Cumberland District, apart from one train each way between Keswick and Penrith, and thus when the LNWR dispensed with 2nd Class carriages and bookings it would be impracticable for the CKPR to act otherwise. The CKPR had no alternative but to give way, and from 1 January 1912 the 1st Class single fare was reduced from 2½d to 2d per mile and the 1st Class return rate was unchanged at 3d per mile; 3rd Class fares were broadly unchanged, and there were no 2nd Class rates.

As already seen, the value of tourist travel was appreciated from the earliest days of the CKPR, but the railway's attitude to excursion traffic, directed at 'day trippers', was ambivalent. Day return fares were featured to a greater or lesser extent through most of the railway's life. In June 1867 the LNWR decided to increase its 'day return' rate from 1½ to 1⅔ times the single fare, but the CKPR Board elected not to follow suit; indeed, they determined to promote excursion traffic and make through bookings to Ullswater, with the hotel proprietors providing transport from Troutbeck station, a journey (from Troutbeck to Patterdale) of about 8 hilly but highly scenic miles, over which connecting coaches were advertised at many periods in CKPR history.

In 1870-71 the CKPR Board had doubts about the wisdom of running excursion trains as such. Because of the perceived risk, the Directors decided not to provide such trains late in the evening. Clearly, their concern was not aroused by the tourists on their select day outings from Keswick to Ullswater; probably the problems arose from drunkenness after closing time. Again, in May 1872, the proposition was to run excursion trains only on special occasions, when the ordinary trains 'would not suit the public'.

Keswick became a favourite destination for long day excursions from the NER, starting very early in the morning from Newcastle-upon-Tyne, Sunderland, Durham, Teesside, Hull or Leeds, and setting off back in the early evening. This traffic was probably at its height in the period from the mid-1880s until about 1914; it contributed to the need and justification for doubling of strategic sections of the route east of Keswick.

Alongside their accelerated development of through express trains to Keswick in Edwardian times, and until 1914-15, the railways were making special efforts to make known the beauties of northern Lakeland more widely. In 1903 photographs were supplied by the CKPR for display in the glazed panels in NER carriages. In 1905 the CKPR contributed to the cost of a large poster featuring coloured scenic views, commissioned by the Keswick Urban District Council. The same year the company's summer timetable introduced pictures of the scenery, McCorquodale & Company of Newton-le-Willows being the printers. This prompted Mrs Edith Rawnsley to paint views of Bassenthwaite and Derwentwater, which she passed to Charles Cropper, a Director of the LNWR and CKPR who had special concern for Lakeland, so that he might arrange further embellishment of the timetable bills.

Mrs Rawnsley was the wife of Canon Rawnsley, of Crosthwaite Church, Keswick and Canon of Carlisle Cathedral, who was a highly respected joint founder of the National Trust (1895); his efforts secured the Trust's first properties in the Lakes. The Canon wrote the CKPR contribution to the LNWR's new illustrated and descriptive guide to the Lake District (1907). The following year, at CKPR request, he wrote a paper with popular appeal describing particularly Brandelhow Woods and Fell (the Trust's first Lakeland property, acquired in 1902) on Derwentwater's shore, and Gowbarrow Park (the second acquisition, in 1906) on the north shore of Ullswater. It is hardly surprising that the Canon's free pass on the railway was renewed; no doubt he used it a great deal in the course of his visits to Carlisle and London on Church and Trust business. The Canon's initiative led to a decision of December 1910 to extend the nameboards of Troutbeck station to read:

Promoting tourist travel, this elaboration of plain 'Troutbeck' was adopted from July 1945. *Courtesy of Abbot Hall*

TROUTBECK FOR ULLSWATER, PATTERDALE GOWBARROW AND AIRA FORCE

It is not quite clear whether this was actually done, but from 3 July 1945 the station nameboards announced:

TROUTBECK FOR ULLSWATER

All this was notwithstanding the fact that the LNWR and LMS were disposed to refer to Penrith as 'the station for Ullswater Lake'.

The LMS was also alive, during the 1920s and 1930s, to the possibilities of long-range excursion trains to the CKPR. Favourite starting points were Blackpool and Morecambe, designed to attract holiday visitors staying in those resorts. The 'round tour' version travelled north over the former Furness Railway's coastal route, commonly with a sojourn at Ravenglass to allow 'all-in' travel by the 15-inch gauge railway up Eskdale and back, then through Workington to reach Keswick for a stay of a few hours, before returning via the Redhills Junction-Eamont Junction LNER curve and the main line over Shap. After the 1929 season, it is believed, these trains ceased to use the Redhills loop line and were reversed in Penrith station; this was a result of the poor condition of the track on the Redhills loop. Similar round-tour day excursions operated for a time in the early 1960s, using DMU sets from as far afield as Stockport and Manchester.

One notes also the opening of the CKPR line on Sundays in summer from the later 1920s until 1939, with the regular day excursions from Glasgow to Keswick and return. On summer Sundays in DMU days, from the later 1950s and even into the 1960s, a regular Newcastle-Carlisle-Penrith-Keswick day excursion train was run; heavily loaded, it sometimes calling for two large locomotives between Penrith and Keswick.

The Glasgow and other Sunday excursions of the 1930s contributed considerably to life in the town of Keswick and its lakeside, and the coaching stock was stabled as far afield as Carlisle and Whitehaven, while the long granite works sidings at Threlkeld were also used for the daytime storage of up to 30 coaches, the equivalent of three substantial excursion train sets.

Period excursions developed from the close ties between folk residing in industrial Workington and its environs and North East England; passenger specials are recalled from West Cumberland to the North East and North Yorkshire at times of local holidays. The Lancashire Fusiliers had a camp near the Motherby-Greystoke road and special trains were run to bring their soldiers to Penruddock station for summer training sessions. Troutbeck was another railhead for 'Territorials' bound for camp. These military specials ran via the Redhills curve, until about 1928-29.

Trains for workmen

More mundane than the outings of Lakes tourists and trippers was the daily to-and-fro of workmen. Such travel could be expected between Cockermouth and Workington and account for the longevity of a daily westbound train from Cockermouth at around 7.20-7.40am. Equally early in origins and long-lived was a passenger train leaving Cockermouth at about 7.00am, eastbound. This would surely be used by workers bound for the pencil manufacturers and other trades in Keswick, but it had also the more long-range function of providing a connection at Penrith for London and intermediate points.

During the First World War a 'workmen's train' was put on from Workington at 8.55pm,

On Sunday 17 July 1960 the 'Newcastle' is about to leave Keswick at 6.30pm, comprising ten corridors worked by '5XP' No 45738 *Samson* and '5MT' No 45286, of Upperby shed. *Harold D. Bowtell*

to Cockermouth, with a return trip at 9.40pm from Cockermouth. In the same period there were also 'colliers trains' from Workington (at 5.00am and 1.05pm) to William Pit Siding, with a balancing working at 5.50am to Workington. Presumably the aim was to provide transport for labour from Whitehaven-Workington to supplement locally resident miners on all three shifts at William Pit, Great Clifton.

The granite quarries at Close, near Embleton, did not enjoy workmen's trains. However, those at Threlkeld not only expanded their local 'quarry village' but also attracted workers from Keswick. By 1906 workmen's trains were running at 6.55am from Keswick to Threlkeld, returning at 12.55pmSO and 5.35pmSX, this service continuing until at least 1929, and probably into the early 1930s. The morning departures varied between 6.50 and 7.05am and the return run started at times that became progressively earlier over the years – 12.50pm, 12.35pm and 12.05pm – on Saturdays. The weekday return was usually timed around 5.30pm in summer, but could be as early as 4.45pm on dark evenings. The train usually comprised one or two coaches and the journey time was of the order of 7-9 minutes. It was known locally as 'The Boer Train', in recognition of the Boer War names assigned to quarry workings opened out around the turn of the century. More light-heartedly, it was alternatively titled 'The Boat Train'.

The platform at Briery Bobbin Mill, in its secluded situation between Keswick and Threlkeld, does not figure on maps or in working timetables in the pre-Grouping era; it was, however, clearly installed early in LMS days and a workers' service from Keswick was provided consistently until about the time of closure of the mill (1958). Indeed, morning and evening calls at this halt (SX) still figured in the BR working timetables of winter 1958-59. The general pattern was to book a call by an up morning passenger train so as to enable workers to arrive by 8.00am. The folk for Briery travelled in the leading coaches in view of the short platform. Return travel was by a passenger train booked to call at lunchtime (SO), or later (SX). There were periods when

calls for workers, bound home to Keswick, were made by the Keswick workmen's train from Threlkeld, and it is believed that there were other periods when a shuttle was run from Keswick to Briery, and at once back again, the locomotive propelling the carriage in one direction.

To school by train
At first sight the CKPR route east of Threlkeld station, climbing hard for all of the 4¼ miles to Troutbeck station, was remote from habitation. It followed the southerly slopes of the valley, which on its northern side is dominated by the great bulk of Blencathra (known colloquially as 'Saddleback') mountain, while the southerly side rises to the high fells of Matterdale Common. There were a considerable number of scattered farmsteads, both below and above the railway; several are farmhouses today, while others are now ancillary premises or purely residences, and a very few are ruinous.

In 1892 local residents had asked for a station to be built near the railway company's Moor Cottages, a pair of small houses, now long combined into one and known as Hill Cottage. The ascending lane to Birkettfield crosses the railway route just west of the cottages, at a point between MP18 and Mosedale viaduct.

By 1900 attention had concentrated on a spot eastward of Mosedale viaduct and MP19, where a lane to upland farms crossed the double-track line by bridge No 91. The tiny signal box named Highgate was on the down side, about 100 yards eastward of the overline bridge, and the company was on the point of building a pair of houses on the up side banking above the line and near the bridge; one was intended for the sole signalman and his family, the other for a section permanent way ganger and family.

Doctor Knight wrote to the company on 4 April 1900 asking for one train each way to call daily at Highgate cabin to pick up and set down six or eight schoolchildren; the Board instructed its Secretary to reply in a typical railway vein that 'the difficulties and expense render the suggestion impracticable'. The children had to walk to and from Mungrisdale school, which was across the valley and some 3 miles to the north of Highgate. Pressure increased, calling for a train service from Highgate to Threlkeld and back; there were indeed suitably timed trains, if only they would call. Many influential folk mustered behind the demand, including the County Council Education Committee, based in Carlisle, and the redoubtable Canon Rawnsley of Keswick.

Towards the end of 1907 the CKPR Board decided to consult the Board of Trade, probably hoping that it would rule against the proposal – but it decided in favour of the suggestion. Thus plans were made, estimated to cost about £170 plus the price of refinements called for by the Board of Trade. Eventually, in February 1908, an agreement was concluded; the Education Committee was to meet the costs of construction and one train each way was to call, initially for ten years. The calls were not to be made 'when the school is closed on holidays or other occasions'.

Colonel Druitt of the railway department at the Board of Trade reported on 18 June 1908 that he had '…inspected the new platforms adjoining Highgate cabin on the CKPR … up and down platforms … 150ft long, 6ft wide, 2ft 6in above rail level, approached by separate pathways from the public road adjoining… Lamps have been provided at the entrance. As the Company do not wish the general public to make any use of the platforms, no nameboards have been provided and the use of the platforms will be restricted to school children only and to one train in the morning and one in the evening. On the conditions, I can recommend sanction.' Approval accompanied the report. Opening followed the summer holiday of 1908, and on Monday 17 August 1908 11 children (12 on 18 August) were conveyed, three joining Threlkeld Council School and nine going to the Quarry School. Highgate platforms became a happy institution in that delightful countryside for the next 20 years.

The site at Highgate is in a cutting and the platforms were staggered, bringing the western end of the down platform close to the signal box. This platform was reached by a fenced path, constructed along the top of the embankment at the level of its access from the road, while the children's path only came down to platform level beside the box on its east side, so that the signalman could watch over their safety. A small waiting hut is recalled, with a stove that the signalman lit on winter mornings. The block post was not switched in until 9.00am in the earlier days,

A rare and wintry scene looking westward at the up platform at Highgate, where children from Threlkeld schools arrived on term-time afternoons (1908-28) before dispersing to their homes at scattered farmsteads. The up home signal can be glimpsed over the bridge, and to the right is the pair of houses built for the railway in 1898. The LNWR 0-6-2T 'Coal tank' is on ballast train duty and Jack Greenhow, ganger in charge of the length, is seen standing on the platform. *Lens of Sutton*

9.30am after about 1908, so the local signalman – the kindly Bob Tinkler, subsequently his successor, Willie Nicholson – was required to put in extra duty and it is believed that the County Council provided a bonus of £5 per annum to cover the time on duty before the call and dispatch of the morning 'school train', which was typically at Highgate just about 8.00am. The signalman was in any case on duty when the afternoon call was made – at about 4.00 to 4.10pm in earlier years, and 3.25pm from about 1917.

The passenger guards also took a kindly interest in their young passengers. One Workington guard, in particular, would invite all the children into his van and make a great show of tabulating their names, then presenting each with sweets. The age range was from five to 14 years, both boys and girls, and a maximum of more than 20 was achieved, thus:

Three from Highgate railway cottages
Five from the families in the Wallthwaite
　community (north-west of the station)
Three from Redsike Farm (north-east of the
　station)
Two from Moorend Farm (northward towards
　the Keswick-Penrith road)
Two from Highgate Close Farm (a little above
　the line, to the south)
Four from Lobbs Farm (higher again)
Three from High Hollows Farm (farther up
　and over to the west of Mosedale Beck)

Attendance was divided between Threlkeld village school – a trek of three-quarters of a mile across the valley from Threlkeld station, sometimes risking wet feet owing to the flooding of the road – and the school in the quarry village, a much shorter and drier trip, made by a select few, among whom notably Jessie Tyson was numbered during the years 1912-19.

By the mid-1920s the number of eligible travellers on the school journey by train, Highgate to Threlkeld, was reduced to rather over half-a-dozen, and from 1926 there was potential competition from a regular bus service between Penrith and Keswick. From 1928 (the end of Christmas term) and officially

with effect from 1 January 1929, the trains ceased to call at Highgate and the youngsters made their way across the fields to a black roadside hut at Red Gate, in order to catch the Cumberland Motor Services Ltd omnibus.

It goes without saying that various social trips, often to Keswick, were made by the trains that called at Highgate platforms. When Jessie Tyson married Ted Titterington on 16 May 1927, they had booked tickets (from Threlkeld to Penrith, and onwards) beforehand and, after a wedding breakfast at Highgate Close, they departed for honeymoon by the school train from Highgate Platform that afternoon.

There were naturally other instances of children travelling by Keswick line trains to and from their schools; indeed, Troutbeck children rode to Penruddock daily, and Keswick School was (and is) of such significance as to draw boys from Cockermouth – note the running, previously discussed, of the M&CR train through to Keswick in the mornings.

Roedean at Keswick, 1940-45
The direct threat posed to the South Coast of England following the German occupation of France in the summer of 1940 led the governors of Roedean School to seek a new home for their prestigious public school and its girls. The elevated and prominent buildings, which face seawards at the easterly extremity of Brighton, were in demand by the army and subsequently passed to a naval shore establishment, HMS Vernon.

The school was found new quarters at Keswick, and this produced unexpected excitements and traffic for the LMS and its Keswick line for five years. The Keswick Hotel, under the management of proprietors Mr and Mrs W. D. Wivell, was occupied by most of the staff and senior girls. Further accommodation was taken in smaller hotels, Millfield and Shu-le-crow, reached by the convenient footbridge over the River Greta. These provided quarters for the junior girls. With all (but one) of the pupils being resident boarders and the staff also to accommodate, it is understood that there was barely a square inch to spare.

In the main building of Keswick station, on its down side (nearest the approach and town), the five upstairs rooms became classrooms; these included the one-time Boardroom of the CKPR and one that was very small and therefore used for special tuition. A waiting room below was also used; some passengers entered and promptly withdrew, whole others were bolder and stayed to enjoy the welcome fire until the arrival of their trains, lessons notwithstanding! Use of a waiting room on the up island platform was also secured in due course. Occasionally, Greek dances were staged on this island platform!

Classrooms were improvised in all three hotels. Notably, the fullest use was made of the covered way from the station's down platform to the Keswick Hotel's side door. Double doors from the platform led into a lobby and further double doors from this to a small decoratively glazed ante-room, which was pressed into use for teaching and known as 'the glass box'. The next glazed door led into a long lounge-conservatory, with windows along one side commanding the station square and, distantly, a view of the mountains. On its other side were the greenhouses. This main lounge was very useful and so were the greenhouses. The school installed laboratory benches, sinks and services. A huge palm tree added dignity to the lounge-conservatory, but leaking glass roofs here and in the greenhouses presented a problem – each mistress and girl required an umbrella in order to cope with the oft-prevailing wet conditions indoors, which reflected the climate of Lakeland and its mountains! A further distraction was the periodic arrival of supplies by rail; the glazed doors would open and a platform trolley would be rumbled through draughtily, accompanied by an aroma of kippers (or whatever!) bound for the kitchens.

Accommodation was also found in the Boardroom of the nearby Fitz Museum and sometimes – shared with visitors – in the adjoining Fitz Art Gallery. The Wesleyan chapel in Southey Street provided for morning prayers and scripture lessons, and its other rooms were used too. Finally, Keswick School offered part-time use of its laboratories to Roedean's sixth form girls. The art mistress probably had the best bargain, commandeering the main garage of the Keswick Hotel and turning it into a magnificent studio and workshop, while another garage housed the bicycles (seemingly one brought by each girl and staff member) much used for outings.

Dame Emmeline Mary Tanner (1876-1955) had been Head of Roedean since 1924 and, wishing to see the school through its wartime era and safely reinstalled at Brighton, she did not retire until Easter 1947. Nancy Banks Smith (*The Guardian*, 17 May 1982), recalling her schooldays at Roedean-in-Keswick, wrote: 'Dame Emmeline's oration "On the Occasion of Two Gels being seen Eating Chips in Keswick" is still spoken of in the same breath as Cato on Catiline...' (Topic: degenerate conspiracy in the Roman Empire.)

Dame Emmeline herself wrote in the school magazine: 'On a perfect October day, 43 girls climbed Great Gable, 16 climbed Scafell Pike, 79 climbed Helvellyn, 16 bicycled to the Langdales (46 miles), 7 walked all round Derwentwater. I was obliged to go to London.' In fact, as well as such outings on Saturdays, school holidays were sometimes given in impromptu fashion, to permit fell and mountain walking on exceptionally fine days.

The railway conveyed Roedean's furniture, equipment and books from Brighton to Keswick in July-August 1940, while the staff arrived during August and the girls on 5 September. Subsequently, a special train was run south at the end of each school term, and north at the beginning of the next. It would be the southbound train of December 1940 – running, it has been suggested, from Keswick through to Brighton – that distinguished itself by arriving far behind booked time. This was during a period of blackout and major air raids, not to mention heavy traffic. The tale in railway circles was that such strident protest came from influential parents, who had awaited their daughters into the cold and dark night hours, that instructions went out to railway staff to ensure that in future the girls' train should have priority over all other wartime traffic – an injunction still recalled in Cumberland in 1945.

The school train seems to have settled down to run from Euston – or a suburban station at periods when heavy air attack was threatened – at around 10.00am, due to arrive at Keswick at approximately 7.00pm. End of term departures from Keswick were booked at 5.25am or 5.30am. This was regarded as the Keswick line's heaviest working in the years 1940-45, one of the few to call for double-heading or even require a 'Black 5' 4-6-0 or other big engine. On one occasion the end of term empty stock, due at Keswick at 5.00am, eventually arrived at 9.00am. In consequence, all the connections at Crewe for south-westerly destinations were missed; much telephoning and many telegrams ensued. Miss Barbara Patterson, teacher of classics and a house-mistress in those days, together with a colleague, took a party from Crewe to Shrewsbury that evening, where they found cramped accommodation for the night. Next day they journeyed on to Exeter, reached about 6.00pm (leaving several girls on the darkened station in the hope that they would be met) and on to Teignmouth. One mistress took the remaining pupil home for the night and saw her off next day for Plymouth and her holidays.

A snowy January resulted in an arrival of the 'school train' from London at about 7.00am at Keswick, 12 hours late; there had not been much heating, nor food (except as provided by individuals) and not even corridor stock. Several girls from other parts of Britain reached Penrith very late on that occasion and were provided with accommodation in the vicinity by the ever-caring station master.

Notable indeed was the universal friendly help of folk in Keswick, starting with Mr and Mrs Wivell, and Dixon the Keswick Hotel porter, who was always ready with weather forecasts and advice about the Lake District. Police Inspector Bell and his colleagues let the school staff know when Derwentwater was safe for skating, which was enjoyed in three winters out of five, with skating by moonlight permitted to the older girls on one superb night. The boatmen readily made their launches available for outings to the further shores, en route for walks or climbs. Keswick station master Pickthall and every one of his staff showed cheerful patience and helpfulness through the five years of 'occupation' of their station by the girls and their mistresses.

The final departure from Keswick was late in 1945. While most of the school staff stayed behind to pack and despatch Roedean's possessions, the girls and a few staff members left on the special 'school train' at 5.25am on 29 November 1945 for a long Christmas holiday, the previous summer holiday having been curtailed to permit this. Everyone was out on the platform in good time, including the Wivells, Dixon, Inspector Bell, many other Keswick friends and especially Mr Pickthall and his staff. Mr Denwood provided music from his loudspeaker van. An informal dance was staged on the platform, and 'John Peel' (a traditional Lakeland song) and 'Auld Lang Syne' were sung. Then the train left on time, accompanied by a fusillade of detonations from the battery of fog signals placed on the outgoing track.

The Keswick Convention

This week-long annual conference of evangelical Christians – of all denominations and attracted from all over the world – remains a feature of summer life in Keswick. It was first held in 1875, its establishment credited to Canon Battersby, Vicar of St John's, Keswick, who died in 1883. The gathering, based in a huge central tent and with overflow to halls in the town, was held in the fourth week of July in the earlier years and into the 20th century, but by the 1930s and subsequently it was staged during the third week in the month, with some breaks in wartime. The atmosphere of 1900 is recalled by reference to the presence in goodly numbers of 'Missionaries to the Heathen'.

The strongest support has come from and via the south of England, with a demand for travel that was first met by the enterprising J. T. Budd, of (significantly) 'Ambleside', New Barnet, Hertfordshire. Commencing in 1899, he advertised 'special train arrangements from London and the South of England to Keswick, on Friday 21 July with return'. The

Above The 'Budd's Special' between London and Keswick for the July interdenominational gathering was always a heavy train. Returning from Keswick on Saturday 21 July 1962, 12 vehicles are here headed by Fowler 2-6-4T No 42357 and Stanier 'Black 5' 4-6-0 No 45190. From 23 November 1964 this direct outlet to the down main line at Penrith No 1 signal box was not available, and all traffic from Keswick had to run thereafter into the CKPR back platform. *Derek Cross*

Below On 22 July 1967 a return Convention special train is seen climbing out of Keswick, hauled by English Electric Type 4 (later Class 40) No D313 and Ivatt Class '4MT' 2-6-0 No 43139. The diesel-electric locomotive ran round the stock at Penrith and worked the train south, bound for Euston. *A. C. Gilbert*

A very rare view of a Class 50 diesel-electric locomotive at work on the Keswick road. Following the downgrading of the truncated Penrith-Keswick section for one-engine working, with all run-round facilities withdrawn, Convention specials were worked on a push-pull basis, with a locomotive at each end of the formation. In July 1969 D417 rounds the curve into Threlkeld at the head of the empty stock of a down Convention special. English Electric Type 4 No D313 is visible at the Keswick end of the train. The carriages were being worked empty to Carlisle. D417 later became No 50017 *Royal Oak*, and was preserved following withdrawal in 1991. D313 subsequently became 40113 and was withdrawn in November 1981. *Peter W. Robinson*

gathering that year was from Monday 24 to Saturday 29 July, and the general pattern was to arrange addresses on Monday evening and at intervals during from Tuesday to Friday. 'The Budd' was sometimes running in two and three portions during the 1920s and 1930s, on a fast daytime schedule from Euston to Penrith, then (reversing direction) assisted in the rear to Blencow or Penruddock, en route to Keswick.

After the 1939-45 war one train sufficed, but this was usually well-loaded and double-headed between Penrith and Keswick. It returned a week later, and in this period, through to 1969, Saturday running in each direction was favoured. The traditional steam working continued until 1967. After that, only a shuttle service between Penrith and Keswick was possible, but the charter train was worked, as shown in the accompanying photograph, by large diesel locomotives at each end of the train, to permit the prompt return of the empty stock.

In CKPR days these special workings to the Keswick Convention, together with others originating in North East England and Scotland, provided a valuable boost in revenue for the Cockermouth Keswick & Penrith Railway Company, but by the 1930s it was the LMS at Euston that gained the financial credit for the induced charter travel to Lakeland's northern railway.

3. Bridges

C&WR: a short line with many river crossings

The route of the Cockermouth & Workington Railway was some 9 miles in length, during which it crossed a major river (the Derwent) six times. Subsidiary channels and tributaries were also crossed. Leaving aside the Derwent viaduct at Workington (used by C&WR trains but owned by the Whitehaven Junction Railway), the C&WR had to commission 11 bridges of nominal lengths of between 50 and 300 feet. The single-track railway was built in 15 months, between February 1846 and April 1847. John Dixon (1796-1865) of Darlington was the Consulting Engineer; he was a respected figure, with experience under George Stephenson on the construction of the Stockton & Darlington and Liverpool & Manchester Railways.

The C&WR was built cheaply, so not only were the intermediate stations of primarily timber construction, but so were the 11 bridges mentioned. John Dixon referred to 'the best timber … of large dimensions' in a progress report of July 1846. By the mid-1850s the vibration of bridges under passing trains was causing concern and in April 1856 William Brown was asked to examine the bridges, in company with J. W. Fletcher, Chairman of the C&WR, and fellow Directors Thomas Westray and George Cape, the last-mentioned probably being a builder by trade.

The resulting report was by William and James Brown, of Whitehaven, and dated 27 May 1856. It stated that most of the C&WR's river bridges required only minor attention, such as realignment of approaching tracks, relaying or reballasting of track on the bridge and the application of a protective finish to the timbers. However, Ribton High bridge (alternatively described as Upper bridge) was found unsafe, calling for the replacement of washed-away piles and other work. In June 1856 tenders for tension rods for this bridge were considered. They were submitted by Piele, Tulk & Ley, Cowan & Sheldon, and G. D. Richardson. The Richardson tender was accepted. Bowling or Low Moor iron was to be used, and by 12 August 1856 the ironwork had been forged at Carlisle and delivery to site was imminent.

Towards the end of the same year, 1856, the C&WR Board took further advice, asking James Dees of the M&CR and WJnR (presumably being the James Dees who joined the C&WR Board in 1863) to inspect the permanent way and state of the line generally. He was also to consider a possible very local doubling between Harrygill and Lowther pit connections, west of Marron, and on Merchants' Quay at Workington. The report by Mr Dees was submitted to the proprietors at their half-yearly meeting on 31 January 1857; it stated that the various timber bridges were standing well and had in many instances been much strengthened and recently improved. However, probably resulting from this review, and also a derailment in March 1857, severe speed limits were imposed over the bridges (from 7 April 1857), namely 10mph for passenger trains and 8mph for coal trains. During that year, William and James Brown were entrusted with more trussing (with iron rods) at Stainburn and Salmon Hall bridges, along with selected water channelling works. The Browns did further work in 1858; the two 42-foot spans at Middle Tail Race bridge and the two 34-foot spans at Tail Race bridge were

Thomas Drane's list of major bridges to be rebuilt, 3 December 1859 (from east to west)

1859 title	LMS title (1940)	Length	Rebuilding progress report (from minutes of 1860-63)
Marron	River Marron (one span)	70ft	Old bridge temporarily strengthened with timber in 1860. At August 1861, to proceed with rebuilding using 'stone piers and iron girders'. Opened January 1862, completed by autumn 1862. *See footnote*
Ribton Hall	Ribton High (two spans)	180ft	At 22 January 1862: both abutments built, a pier still to be constructed. 29 July 1862: traffic was passing over new bridge.
Ribton Hall No 2	Ribton (six spans)	300ft	At 1859: 'recently strengthened with iron trussing rods'. 31 January 1861: rebuilding authorised. At 9 April 1861: tenders accepted – W. Hodgson for masonry, Gilkes, Wilson & Co for iron girders. At 11 June 1861: stone piers in hand. At 22 January 1862: rails to be laid this week. At 29 July 1862: No 2 coffer dam commenced.
Camerton	Camerton (three spans)	270ft	At 1859: 'recently strengthened with iron trussing rods'. At 22 January 1862: one abutment complete, one abutment and three piers to build (*I would only expect two piers – Author*). At 29 July 1862: track being laid.
Table top	Stainburn (two spans)	165ft	At 9 April 1861: tenders accepted (as for Ribton). At 22 January 1862: abutments complete, centre pier to build. At 7 July 1862: track being laid.
Salmon Hall	Salmon Hall No 1 (three spans)	165ft	At 1859: 'recently strengthened with iron trussing rods'. At 22 January 1862: abutments in progress, one pier to build (*implying one built – Author*). At 29 July 29 1862: traffic passing over new bridge.
Salmon Hall No 2	Salmon Hall No 2 (two spans)	120ft	At 22 January 1862: masonry complete, girders to fix. At 29 July 1862: traffic passing.
Salmon Hall Byefall	Byefalls (two spans)	90ft	At 11 June 1861: work in hand, a stone pier in mid-stream. At 22 January 1862: 'completed'. At 29 July 1862: traffic passing.
Canal	Mill Race (one span)	60ft	At 31 January 1861: decided to rebuild Mill Race bridge. At 22 January 1862: abutments completed and girders to fix for 'Mill Race' (*presumed to refer to this bridge – Author*). At 29 July 1862: traffic passing over 'Mill Race.'
Canal No 2	Canal (one span)	60ft	At 31 January 1861: decided to rebuild 'Boat bridge'. At 22 January 1862: 'completed'. At 29 July 1862: traffic crossing.
Beerpot (stated to cross tail race for Beerpot Ironworks)	Beerpot Mill Race (one span)	50ft	At 15 July 1862: decided on permanent rebuilding (over tail race at Beerpot). At January 1863: rebuilding in hand; last bridge in programme. At 4 July 1863: opened.

Notes:
The lengths are as quoted by Drane

Mr Harrison Hodgson, of Durham, undertook the contracts for masonry for Marron, Ribton Hall, Ribton Hall No 2, Camerton, Table Top, Salmon Hall No 1 and Salmon Hall No 2 - in April 1861 and July 1861. It is not clear whether he also carried out the masonry work for the four more westerly bridges. The wrought iron girders for all the bridges were provided by Gilkes Wilson & Company, who would be of Middlesbrough, under orders of April and June 1861. One notes that the rails were laid and traffic commenced to pass over some of the new bridges before the final completion of intermediate river piers.

The 1861 reference to Marron Bridge may well refer to stone abutments and iron girders (*Author*)

Ribton Hall No 2, subsequently retitled Ribton Bridge, No 22, was rebuilt in 1862 with six spans (carried by stone abutments and piers) varying between 32 and 38 feet, and with an overall length of 300 feet. It was the longest of the C&WR's succession of bridges over the River Derwent, seen here probably in the 1930s. *Richard L. Pattinson/CRA*

noted for trussing, and two piles were to be fixed each side of the trusses on Beer Pot Tail Race bridge.

The railway's mineral traffic was gradually increasing, with promise of continued development, and it was realised that the timber structures of 1846-47 must be coming to the end of their useful lives. Accordingly, a major report was commissioned. It was dated 3 December 1859, at Cockermouth, by Thomas Drane CE, who was by then Engineer of the C&WR.

All the indications are that each of the original timber bridges was supported on numerous timber piles, on piled foundations in the riverbed, the spans between them being comparatively short. Mr Drane's report of 1859 listed 11 timber bridges and recommended their rebuilding, using wrought iron girders for the superstructure, with spans of typically 50-60 feet, in order to minimise the number of piers obstructing the river. In general, the girders would be supported by masonry abutments, supplemented by masonry piers in the stream, as required. The piers were to be erected in water conditions of 'low summer'. Ribton Hall bridge (which would be the one known also from time to time as Ribton Upper or Ribton High) would need iron piling for the piers, in view of the depth of water. All abutments and piers would be of adequate width for double track, but only one pair of girders, for single track, would be installed for each span at this time. The Engineer's estimate for the full scheme, to be spread over several summers, was £6,500, which was very different from the individual expenditures of £11-£113 for the repair work previously carried out by Browns on the timber structures. Nevertheless, the Board accepted Mr Drane's recommendations and the first work was put in hand in the spring of 1860. The bridge over the Marron and those over the Derwent were all completed by autumn 1862. The new Beerpot bridge was opened to traffic on 4 July 1863 and this was stated to eliminate all timber bridges on the C&WR – although a small timber bridge near Broughton Cross station was seemingly not rebuilt with iron girders until 1865.

Doubling of the C&WR route and its bridges

The Whitehaven Junction Railway provided double track between Workington joint station and Derwent Junction (the divergence of the C&WR's own route), but the first serious reference to prospective double line between Derwent Junction and Cockermouth appears to have been in December 1856, when local doubling was considered in the vicinity of the colliery branches near Marron. Doubling from Workington (meaning Derwent Junction) to the River Marron was contemplated by the estimate of £14,500 put to a special meeting on 28 October 1862; this meeting authorised the seeking of parliamentary powers for various works, and an Act was secured on 30 June 1863. However, the first Ordnance Survey of the route, in 1864, found not even the 1856 project executed. There was simply a double line, or crossing loop, of just about one quarter-mile in length, between the junctions for Harrygill Colliery and for Linefitts Colliery, inclusive. This took in, intermediately, Marronbridge Junction (the later Marron Junction, West) and the station site. There could also be limited stowage of mineral trains on the southerly branch line from Marron (west) or the several industrial connections, of which the one at Melgramfitz Colliery (operational from November 1863) was double-ended.

Following an estimate of £2,500 (provided for on 23 February 1864), on 5 April 1864 a tender was seemingly accepted for doubling 'from the east end of Ribton High bridge to Melgram Fitz Colliery', about 1 mile, and including the already existing quarter-mile of double road. The only major bridge involved was at Marron, and Gilkes provided a girder for its widening, also under order of April 1864. It is believed that the work was done that year.

Doubling from Workington Bridge station to Derwent Junction had been mooted for some time and was doubtless carried out in the first half of 1865, as a relevant addition to capital was made at a general meeting of 29 July 1865.

Widening between Lowther Pit and Workington Bridge – involving extra girders over all the other recently built major bridges – was held over (decision of 9 May 1865), and Melgramfitz to Cockermouth Junction was not seriously considered at the time. This was the position when the LNWR took over, midway through 1866. In fact, the LNWR was quick to widen the remaining bridges and the C&WR main line, to achieve double track throughout. The demands of M&CR traffic between Brigham and Cockermouth Junction led to this portion being given priority, being opened to traffic even before its inspection for the Board of Trade. The section from Brigham westward to Melgramfitz was ready on that date and clearly opened as double line soon afterwards. The length from the vicinity of Lowther Pit to the approaches to Workington Bridge station (including the remaining major underline bridges) was opened as double track very soon after inspection on 5 October 1868.

Improvement to stations in the C&WR era, to 1865

Work on the C&WR's Cockermouth station was under way in September 1856, when George Cape (a Director, presumed to be a builder) undertook to see to the foundations, for which the bricks were already on site. Workington Bridge and Camerton stations were provided with platforms, in front of the old buildings, around autumn 1860.

New and worthy buildings for Broughton Cross and Brigham stations were erected between March and the autumn of 1863 by

H. Hodgson, whose tender for the work had been £738. Both were in neo-Elizabethan style, built in stone with steep-pitched gables and heavy roofing; the Broughton Cross building can still be seen today, beside the A66 road. Camerton, remote from habitation, was also to have a 'permanent' new station building (1863), but this was held over in 1863-65 and the eventual building was very different from those of 1863.

Marron Junction platform and shed were built in 1866 at the C&WR's cost, but the WC&ER had to make annual contributions. Workington Bridge station did not benefit from new buildings until 1881, a modest rebuilding in wood by the LNWR.

Bridges from Cockermouth to Workington, 1866-1966

The principal bridges of 1847 to 1859 have already been tabulated, and their rebuilding during 1860-63 has also been discussed, as has the doubling of the line in 1864-65 and 1867-68.

The bridges, as they stood during most of the century of successively LNWR, LMS and BR control, are listed clearly in the LMS register compiled in the 1940s and much of this is reproduced in the following table. Most are underline bridges, the few overline being distinguished. Stone abutments and stone piers are universal except in a few instances noted in the table: for example, C&WR No 43 (a footbridge) and various Whitehaven Junction Railway structures. Underline cattle-creeps and culverts and the occasional accommodation or public way – mainly under 10-foot span – are omitted from the table; most of them comprised stone abutments and stone arches but a few had stone abutments with cast iron girders and infill planking. As viewed by the engineers of LMS days and after, the Derwent bridges of the C&WR line were unduly light in superstructure. The wrought iron cross girders under the double track road deflected significantly under the load of a train, causing the longitudinal wrought iron girders to lift at their ends, where supported by abutments or piers at the end of each span. The prospective cost of replacing these superstructures in steel was an ever-looming factor – and perhaps not justified in the 1960s.

Bridges between Cockermouth and Workington, 1866-1966

No	Between stations	MPs	Title	No of spans between abutments or piers/length (skew)	Remarks
7	Cockermouth Jn Brigham	1.25/1.5	Thompson's Arch (underline)	1/12ft	
10	Brigham Broughton Cross	2.25/2.5	Stoney Beck Broughton Road	1/17ft 4in (20ft 9in) over stream; 1/25ft 7in (30ft 6in) over public way; 1/17ft 1in (20ft 10in) over occupation way	WI girders and planking; CI face girders to Up line; stone arches under Down line. Lost in A66 redevelopment.
12	Broughton Cross Marron Junction	2.75-3	Paisley's Arch (underline occupation)	1/12ft	Lost in A66 redevelopment.
13	Broughton Cross Marron Junction	2.75-3	Cattle creep	1/13ft (14ft)	Lost in A66 redevelopment.

No	Between stations	MPs	Title	No of spans between abutments or piers/length (skew)	Remarks
16	Broughton Cross Marron Junction	3.75-4	River Marron	1/53ft 6in	WI main and cross girders and planking. Span survived in 1984.
20	Marron Junction Camerton	4.25-4.5	Ribton High (over Derwent)	1/66ft (72ft 4in); 1/63ft (73ft)	WI main and cross girders and planking. Spans removed.
22	Marron Junction Camerton	4.5-4.75	Ribton (over Derwent)	1/38ft (46ft) over occupation way; 1/34ft (42ft) over river; 1/36ft 4in (44ft 6in) over island; 1/32ft 6in (44ft 3in) over river; 1/32ft (40ft 3in) over river; 1/34ft (42ft 6in) over river.	WI main and cross girders and planking. All spans removed since 1966 closure.
25	Marron Junction Camerton	5-5.25	Camerton (over Derwent)	1/50ft 8in (62ft 8in); 1/56ft 6in (70ft 2in); 1/50ft (63ft 4in)	Construction as Ribton. West abutment partly rebuilt in concrete in 1948. All spans removed since 1966 closure.
26	South of Camerton Station (which closed 3 March 1952)	5-5.25	Footbridge over Derwent	1/40ft 2in; 1/ 40ft 5in; 1/ 39ft 10in; 1/39ft 4in	Timber bridge giving access from south to station; sold 1 June 1959 to Cumberland County and since replaced.
28	Camerton Workington Bridge	5.5-5.75	Miser (overline, byroad to St Peter's Church)	1/30ft; 2/16ft	Broad stone arch over double track, flanked by arches set into sides of cutting.
30	Camerton Workington Bridge	at 5.75	Stainburn (over Derwent)	2/66ft (71ft 9in)	WI main and cross girders and planking. Timber decking (Up side renewed 1964). Spans removed since 1966 closure.
31	Camerton Workington Bridge	5.75-6	William Pit (overline)	1/29ft over occupation way; 1/17ft over Allerdale Coal Company	WI lattice girders and plates for occupation span; 17ft span had steel beams, concrete floor, corrugated iron parapets, stone and brick abutments. Whole structure sold in 1979; since demolished

No	Between stations	MPs	Title	No of spans between abutments or piers/length (skew)	Remarks
33	Camerton Workington Bridge	6-6.25	Salmon Hall No 1 (over Derwent)	1/41ft 8in (52ft); 1/38ft 6in (49ft 6in); 1/44ft 8in (53ft)	WI main and cross girders and planking. All spans removed since 1966 closure. Two river piers demolished c1983.
34	Camerton Workington Bridge	6.6.25	Salmon Hall No 2 (over a Derwent channel)	1/44ft 3in (50ft); 1/34ft 4in (38ft)	Construction as for Salmon Hall No 1. Both spans removed since 1966 closure.
36	Camerton Workington Bridge	6.25-6.5	Byefalls (over a Derwent channel)	1/25ft 6in (40ft 4in); 1/29ft (39ft 2in)	Construction as for Salmon Hall bridges. Both spans removed since 1966 closure.
37	Camerton Workington Bridge	6.25-6.5	Mill Race (over canal from Derwent to Seaton Mill and Beerpot Works)	1/41ft (57ft 6in)	Construction as for Salmon Hall bridges. Span removed since 1966 closure. Seaton corn mill was just south of line and became a farm by c1930.
39	Camerton Workington Bridge	6.5-6.75	Canal (being above canal but downstream of mill race; served Beerpot Works)	1/34ft (59ft 4in)	Construction as for Salmon Hall, etc; very much on skew. Water since piped and site largely filled in.
41	Camerton Workington Bridge	6.75-7	Beerpot(over former mill race, old Beerpot Works to Derwent)	1/16ft (29ft)	A very skew bridge, steel beams and floor plates; with concrete jack-arches as reconstructed in 1896. Survived in 1984.
42	At Workington Bridge Station	7.25-7.5	Calva (overline carrying public road)	1/26ft (28ft)	Steel girders and brick jack-arches. Significantly reconstructed in 1960.
43	At Workington Bridge Station	7.25-7.5	Passenger footbridge (over-line)	1/39ft	WI lattice girders and planking. Station closed 1 January 1951 and bridge subsequently removed.
44	Workington Bridge-Derwent Jn	7.25-7.5	'LMSR' over LNWR, but generally known as 'navvies bridge'	1/49ft (57ft)	WI girders and planking. Bridge No 49 in CWJR line schedule. Maintenance transferred to Workington Corporation after closure.

No	Between stations	MPs	Title	No of spans between abutments or piers/length (skew)	Remarks
45A	Workington Bridge Derwent Jn	7.75-8	Highway viaduct (B5298 over line)	1/53ft 7in	Steel main and cross girders and plates. Maintained by Workington Corporation.

Bridges on the section of route over the Whitehaven Junction line, Derwent Junction to Workington Main Station

No	Between stations	MPs	Title	No of spans between abutments or piers/length (skew)	Remarks
37	Derwent Jn Workington	7-7.25	Derwent Viaduct (over tidal mouth of Derwent)	8/No 1 43ft (45ft 9in); Nos 2-4 each 35ft (44ft); Nos 5-7 each 44ft 9in (56ft); No 8 43ft 9in (55ft)	Stone abutments; piers of WI cylinders each 6ft 1in diameter and filled with brick in cement; steel main girders; footway on Up (west) side – since reconstructed.
36	Derwent Jn Workington (at junction of Merchants Quay branch)	7-7.25	Public footbridge (overline)	1/42ft 3in	Stone piers, WI lattice girders and timber decking; timber steps renewed in concrete in 1960s.
35	Derwent Jn Workington	6.75-7	Harbour (Brewery Beck) (over tidal water)	1/32ft (32ft 5in)	Brick abutments, steel longitudinal girders, brick jack-arches and concrete floor.
33	Derwent Jn Workington	6.75-7	South Quay (public road over line)	2/No 1 26ft 5in (S end), 35ft 9in (N end) over main line; No 2 25ft over goods lines	Stone abutments, stone piers, WI girders and floor plates. Bridge maintained by Corporation.
32	At Workington Main Station	6.75-7	Passenger footbridge (overline)	1/60ft 11in; 2/10ft 1.5in over platform	CI columns, WI lattice girders, timber floor.

Notes: WJnR Nos 37-32 are on a line still open today, unlike the structures that survive on the C&WR or CWJR.

Note that the river bridges on the C&WR route all appear to reconcile with those rebuilt 1860-63, as widened subsequent to original construction in order to accommodate a double line of way.

Bridges on the C&WR route have been presented in order of the Railway's numbering, east to west (Cockermouth Junction to Derwent Junction), whereas those on the CKPR will be taken west to east, in the Up direction, in line with their numbering and the mileposts on the route.

Bridges on the CKPR line

Just as the 9-mile C&WR route was notable for the number and dimensions of its bridges, so the 31 miles of the CKPR could claim similar distinction, also displaying a number of highly individual designs. These were mostly evolved by its Engineer, Thomas (later Sir Thomas) Bouch during the building of the line in the years 1862-64. The route was in a superb setting and involved negotiation of mountain streams, fast-rising and swift-flowing rivers and often-flooded pastures. Thomas Bouch had only recently completed the Stainmore route, designed to carry Durham coke to Furness and Cumberland and including among its works the lofty, spidery and quite spectacular iron viaducts at both Belah and Deepdale. It is interesting that nowhere on the CKPR route did the obstacles take the form of the deep ravines found on the Stainmore crossing of the Pennines. Had it been so, the appropriate drawings might have been taken out in Edinburgh, dusted and adapted. However, Bouch adopted various standard designs for his CKPR structures, but the designs were of quite different standards, to suit widely differing locations on the route. The following may be distinguished:

1 Underline bridges with wrought iron trough girder spans of up to 20 feet between their stone abutments, the transverse joists being also of wrought iron. One 25-foot span is noted, but that incorporated concrete jack arches and would probably date from works of 1901-02. Bridge No 134 (over the NER double track near Redhills) was of 36ft 6in span, employing wrought iron main girders and cross girders, but this may have been of NER design and construction.

2 Overline bridges having wrought iron girder spans on stone abutments, with jack arches and tie rods beneath the carriageway in the original design and finished off by the insertion of delightful cast iron railings in the parapet walls beside the road.

3 Handsomely proportioned stone arched bridges, with stone abutments and sometimes with wing walls, for both overline and underline spans of up to about 20 feet.

4 Comparable stone arched underline bridges of rather greater span.

5 Underline viaducts with several arches (for example, 12 arches over Mosedale) of around 22-30-foot individual arch spans, the structures being in masonry but with the actual arches sometimes in brick. I have not established whether the brick arches were original or introduced during the reconstruction works of the 1890s.

6 The screw-piled underline bridges. These were commonly (but not invariably) employed in crossing low-lying lands subject to flooding and are seen between Braithwaite and Keswick, also at bridge 78, Screw Ghyll, over the Glenderamachin river. Cast iron piles, threaded at the foot, were screwed into the ground using a suspended augur or 'whim' type of tool, then built up by superimposing and bolting cast iron tubular columns to achieve the desired height. Each pier was formed of a pair of these columns, of 12-inch diameter, inserted and set up transversely to the line of the route and connected by light diagonal stays. The span between the piers was typically of 23-24 feet, having cast iron side girders and timber transverse joists, timber longitudinals and timber decking, the whole stiffened by 1¼-inch-diameter iron tie rods in the timber floor. The width across each twin pier and the superstructure was adequate for a single line of railway, never double track in the CKPR examples of this construction. Stone abutments were located at the ends of these multiple-span bridges.

7 Bowstring girder underline bridges of wrought iron construction, on land-based stone abutments, each bridge a single span of 64-119 feet and with no intermediate piers. The 64-foot (upright) span was in bridge No 47 over the Derwent. Spans of 80-119 feet were employed for the river bridges in the Greta gorge between Keswick and the Glenderamachin. Of these, three have upright bowstring side girders (the curved boom being above rail level) and four employ inverted 'bowstrings' (with the curved boom below rail level). The range of span is much the same for each type. It is suggested that Bouch preferred the inverted arrangement but clearance above the river bed and high water was not in all cases adequate to permit this arrangement.

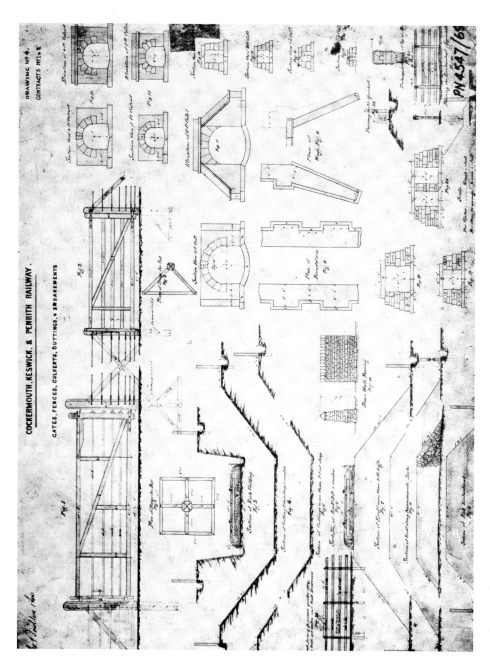

A selection of culverts, smaller bridges, fences, gates, embankments and cuttings – drawn and signed by 'Thomas Bouch, CE' and his contractors 'Geo Boulton & Son'. *Courtesy of Chief Civil Engineer, BR/LMR*

A contemporary Teesside name of the 1860s, seen embellishing an underline accommodation bridge near Embleton. *Richard L. Pattinson/CRA*

8 Single-span overline bridges of substantial length, for example 60 feet, with slightly arched lattice side girders and (originally) timber transverse joists and timber decking, the bridges springing from stone abutments set in the upper part of the sides of. cuttings. These structures (seemingly eight in number) were primarily intended for 'accommodation' use between farmers' fields and suitable only for restricted loads. That giving access to Threlkeld Quarry was the one most severely treated and it still carries some road traffic today; steel transverse joists were substituted at some date in its history. These are bridges of graceful, almost airy, appearance and have been informally styled 'birdcage bridges' or 'fly bridges'.

It is believed that all these designs date from Bouch's work as Engineer and that of Boulton as the original contractor to the CKPR – although original drawings have not been found in all cases.

The widening of the line to double track between Threlkeld and Troutbeck in 1893-94 involved the rebuilding of several overline road bridges. An interesting standard was adopted for this work, employing deep, cast iron outer girders to a curved profile and four intermediate straight webbed girders, on stone abutments. Brick jack arches, each of 4-foot or so span and five in number, typically completed the deck, which supported the foundation 'puddle' for a carriageway, which was about 20 feet wide between parapets. It was a late date for the use of cast iron in new bridgeworks, albeit these were not underline

bridges; steam road vehicles could well be required to cross them. The only underline bridge not of masonry/brick arch construction on the section doubled in 1893-94 was No 86 (Guard House) of nearly 20 feet span, and here steel girders were employed. By the time the doubling was extended from Troutbeck to Penruddock (1900-01), the CKPR's Engineer was employing steel girders and concrete jack arches for underline bridges crossing roads. In LMS and BR days, reinforced concrete was prominent in new bridgeworks on the route, particularly in the construction of bridge decks.

The CKPR line was thus notable for the aesthetic and technical interest of its bridges – but it was also notorious for the amount of trouble and anxiety that many of them caused throughout the 101 years of its existence as a through route, from 1865 to 1966. The earlier study of timetables and train working shows that this was never a heavily used route for minerals, goods or passengers, nor did speeds range high.

In December 1885 the Board of Trade asked for a report on iron underline bridges, but the company's Board, realising their weakness, resolved (January 1886) on a non-committal reply, and they were not pressed by the Board of Trade. Their Permanent Way Committee was at this time already expressing its concern about the screw-pile bridges. John Wood had been resident engineer under Bouch during the CKPR's construction and had been Company Engineer from the opening of the line. He was authorised by the Board (in February 1886) to substitute wrought iron cross girders for the wood beams in one span of the screw-pile bridges. One wonders whether this decision is correctly recorded. Should it not point to putting *one* wrought iron cross girder in *each* span of the relevant bridges?

The near-flimsy construction of the CKPR's screw-pile bridges, the relatively light dimensions of the long-span bowstring girder bridges, and developing defects in the arched viaducts were not major problems until the new century, as meanwhile the LNWR 'Special DX' and NER '1001' 0-6-0 locomotives had jogged contentedly to and fro, with a maximum of no more than 35 tons or so spread over three coupled axles.

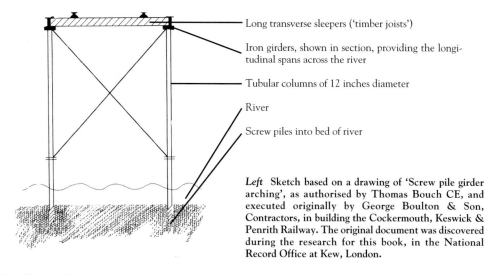

Long transverse sleepers ('timber joists')

Iron girders, shown in section, providing the longitudinal spans across the river

Tubular columns of 12 inches diameter

River

Screw piles into bed of river

Left Sketch based on a drawing of 'Screw pile girder arching', as authorised by Thomas Bouch CE, and executed originally by George Boulton & Son, Contractors, in building the Cockermouth, Keswick & Penrith Railway. The original document was discovered during the research for this book, in the National Record Office at Kew, London.

Below The troublesome multi-span bridges, carried on cast iron columns and screw piles, figured mainly between Braithwaite and Crosthwaite, their numbers within the range 39-51. This LMS drawing (undated, but probably of 1936) shows the upper portion of a pair of original 12-inch-diameter cast iron columns of 1863-64, still in use and tied together by original diagonal iron stays, of which the dimensions and form are apparent. It is bridge No 41 (Newlands Beck) and the steel girder span shown was installed in 1914 (or slightly later) to replace the original transverse timber joists that had been supported by cast iron side girders and strengthened by 1¼-inch-diameter iron tie rods in the timber floor. The columns were still based on screw piles in the 1930s. *J. M. Hammond collection/Carlisle Record Office*

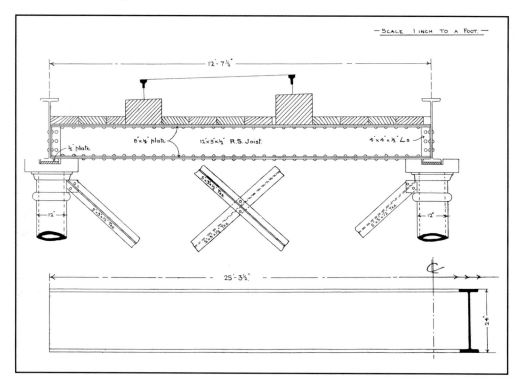

Above Between Keswick and Threlkeld could be found a series of mostly bowstring girder spans in wrought iron, within the Greta gorge. This is Stank Dub, bridge No 59, at Keswick, viewed upstream into the gorge. The bridge is formed of a pair of inverted bowstrings, of 113ft 6in span. They were strengthened in 1933 with a massive steel centreplate girder (see page 70). *Harold D. Bowtell*

Below White Moss bridge, No 69, is an upright bowstring, with an 80-foot skew span, seen here looking west. No spectacular strengthening is reported but four supplementary transverse understruts extend as outriggers and carry stays to stiffen the main bowstrings. *Harold D. Bowtell*

Bridge No 87 at Hill Cottage, looking east, is seen as rebuilt for doubling of the line, with cast iron side members that carry the raised inscription 'PRATCHITT BROTHERS CARLISLE 1893'. The abutments and parapet walls are in masonry with brick barrel (or 'jack') arches between the cast side members. *Harold D. Bowtell*

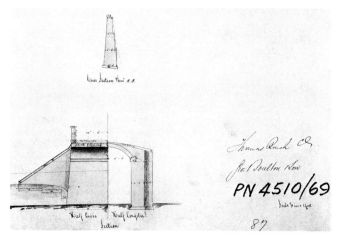

This is part of an original drawing for bridge No 87, then for single line, by Bouch and Boulton. *Courtesy of Chief Civil Engineer, BR/LMR*

In 1901 the NER built its first eight-coupled mineral locomotive, the 'T' Class, with more than 58 tons carried by four coupled axles, and in February 1904 NER Locomotive Superintendent Wilson Worsdell wrote to suggest running these engines through to Cockermouth with the coke trains. John Wood joined Peter Thompson, CKPR Secretary and General Manager, in meeting Vincent Raven, Assistant to Mr Worsdell, to discuss this proposition. Prompted by his Board, Mr Thompson then wrote to enquire whether the NER would help with the cost of necessary bridgeworks. This brought a response from NER General Manager George S. Gibb, who replied sternly, indeed with asperity, suggesting that it was the responsibility of the CKPR as a revenue-earning concern to renew its own bridges!

In 1906 the issue was still live, with the NER wishing to run the 'T' locomotives through and also now asking for the 'C' and 'C1' Class 0-6-0 engines to run over the line, probably on excursions from the North East to Keswick. A meeting was held at Penrith with Messrs Thompson, Wood (by now engineering consultant) and A. M. Bristow (the newly appointed Engineer) representing the CKPR, while Messrs Smeddle (District Locomotive Superintendent, Darlington) and Bengough were the NER representatives. The proposition was to run the 'C' engines for a few months and monitor the effect on rails and bridges. In July 1906 the CKPR agreed to spend £60 on work necessary to allow the 'C' engines, but in August, following costings by Mr Wood, the Board decided not to undertake strengthening of bridges for the much heavier

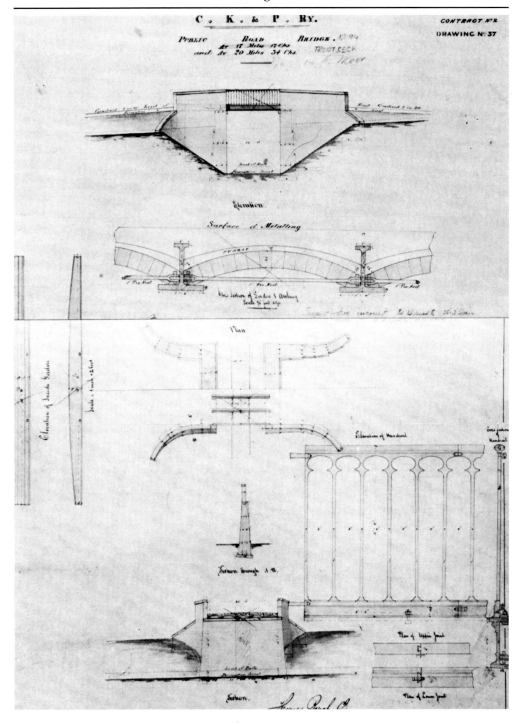

It is good to see these original Bouch/Boulton drawings of Gibson bridge (No 94), located east of MP20, between Highgate and Troutbeck. Observe the delicate cast iron handrails, inset in the parapet wall, and the jack arches below the carriageway. *Courtesy of Chief Civil Engineer, BR/LMR*

Looking past the catch points, westwards down the bank between Troutbeck and Threlkeld, accommodation bridge No 90 is seen spanning the running lines, doubled after 1890. *Richard L. Pattinson/CRA*

This more detailed study of 'birdcage' accommodation bridge No 90 (near MP19), with its timber floor retained, is dated c1924 and shows construction details. Jessie Titterington (then Tyson) is seen with Fly and Bess. Her family farmed at Highgate, close by. The question arises as to whether this bridge was reconstructed or renewed for the doubling of this section of line in the 1890s. *Jessie Titterington collection*

'T' Class 0-8-0s. Consequently the NER settled down to running 'P' or 'P1' 0-6-0s, little heavier than the old '1001', on its mineral trains over the CKPR. Presumably the larger-wheeled 'C' Class mixed-traffic type came in on special passenger trains. Meanwhile, the LNWR was content to run 'Special DX' and '18-inch Goods' (alias 'Cauliflowers') – both lighter locomotives than their NER contemporaries – on passenger and goods trains.

Around 1912 some work (not radical) was done on the screw-pile bridges. Subsequently, with the permission of the LNWR's General Manager, the District Engineer for the Company's Northern District, Mr Thurstan, based at Lancaster, was invited to report on civil engineering aspects of the CKPR. This was in May 1913 and his reports were forthcoming between July and September

1913. Mr Thurstan recommended infilling the screw-pile bridges between Braithwaite and Keswick so far as practicable and strengthening those spans retained to cope with streams or flood waters. Meanwhile, in November 1913, a speed limit of 45mph was imposed over the whole length of the CKPR. This probably caused no inconvenience for the slow mineral and goods trains, but it could cramp the downhill style of the sprightly 2-4-0 'Jumbo' passenger engines, which were then coming into use on the line. In January 1914 the CKPR Engineer issued a list of screw-pile bridges for partial filling and strengthening: Nos 41, 48-51 and 78 (Screw Ghyll/ Glenderamachin). No 41 was tackled at once.

The committee on bridges walked the line from Braithwaite to Keswick in April 1914 and their recommended list for attention on this section embraced Nos 39, 40, 42-45 and 48-50. The committee at this time had an eye to heavier locomotives and the tendency for subsidence of screw-piled columns under railway loadings – as distinct from those of, for example, seaside piers, which were built in similar style. They suggested that extra intermediate columns set on concrete bases be provided – but in fact this course was never adopted by the CKPR.

Work proceeded during the years 1914-19 on the above-mentioned bridges. In 1918 the railway received vociferous complaints from landowners concerning flooding attributed to infilling at bridge No 43 (Watery Lane, near MP11, north of Braithwaite); an additional element of flood relief was then introduced. Filling of screw-pile bridges was resumed after an interval of nearly ten years, in 1928 and 1930 – and total reconstruction took place in 1935, 1936 and 1938; No 78 (Screw Ghyll) was replaced by a single-span steel bridge, while the others in this period were rebuilt in steel or reinforced concrete. Finally there was work in 1950 and 1955. In filling, the usual practice was to remove the old superstructure and tip 'fill' material, burying the piers in the resulting embankment, commonly with one modern bridge span or just a penetrating culvert (for flood relief) retained. In retrospect, how much easier it would have been to adopt the 'embankment with culverts' approach in 1862-64.

The lofty multiple-arched viaducts also caused anxiety and the resultant work was primarily seen at Penruddock, Mosedale and Cockermouth. At Penruddock, after urgent inspection by Mr Thurstan of the LNWR at Lancaster, five arches were filled in the 1918-20 period. At Mosedale viaduct, buttressing of arches, particularly in 1943-44, was carried out and is self-evident today. Inadequate thickness and strength in the spandrel walls above the arches prompted the insertion of transverse tie rods in many arches, notably at Mosedale. The Cocker arched viaduct was converted during 1944-45 to a three-span bridge of reinforced concrete beams. The specialised services of Leonard Fairclough, a Lancashire contractor experienced in concrete work, was enlisted for this job. The casting and curing of pre-cast concrete beams was done on an adjacent site, and the LMS brought large cranes from Crewe and Horwich. It will be observed that crises tended to develop inconveniently during the difficult days of both world wars of the 20th century.

There is a hint on record that work was in hand on bowstring girder bridges in the Greta gorge in 1897, and No 73 (Rowsome) was

Out of the Greta gorge at last: this is Screw Ghyll (alternatively Glenderamachin or Glenderamackin) bridge No 78, which had cast iron columns on screw piles and six spans but was rebuilt as seen in 1936. The new bridge featured a single 77-foot steel span of riveted construction between abutments of concrete, with stone facings; it has a floor of rolled steel joists and concrete and is seen from the southerly side. Threlkeld station is not far to the right. *Harold D. Bowtell*

A general view of Mosedale viaduct, bridge No 89; it had masonry abutments and 12 brick arches, each of 29ft 4in span, of which the left (easterly) one is almost hidden. *Harold D. Bowtell*

Penruddock viaduct (bridge No 105) east of the station of that name. As seen, this featured four arches of 25ft 3in apiece, but had been built with nine arches; Nos 1-5 (nominally) were filled in the period 1918-20. This structure was never widened. The view is from the south-east. *Harold D. Bowtell*

fitted with additional cross girders in 1905. The problem with the CKPR bridges of this type was simply that they were not of sufficiently robust design for the locomotives that the LMS of the 1920s and 1930s wished to run over the route from Penrith to Keswick and beyond. The NER/LNER coke traffic had declined to virtually nothing by 1925, but the LMS was then looking at tourist potential for the route and it was probably around this time that the Chief (Civil) Engineer promised the Chief General Superintendent (the senior commercial and operating officer) that he would reconstruct, strengthen or eliminate at least one weak bridge each year on the CKPR/C&WR route, with priority for the Penrith-Keswick section. The bowstring bridges were consequently dealt with in 1925 (No 73), 1928 (No 74), 1929 (Nos 67 and 71), 1931 (Nos 66 and 75) and 1933 (No 59). No 69 required no substantial works. Each reconstruction was a major operation, typically

involving a long weekend line possession, the new components being prepared and brought to the site in advance, so far as space permitted, while two or three cranes were in attendance for the selected weekend.

In the upright bowstring girders, the curved upper flange is the compression flange or boom and an inherent weakness in the original design was the inadequate bracing of these flanges. Transverse stays could be installed between the pair of curved upper flanges if the depth was sufficient to do this, while clearing the loading gauge for passage of trains below the stays – and in any case these stays could only be placed towards the centre of the span. This practice was adopted by LMS engineers but its limitations explain why the universal method followed was to install transverse cross girders below the bowstrings and under the bridge deck, with these girders extending as 'outriggers' from which rigid stays (superficially reminiscent of the much

Above This view of Rowsome, bridge No 73 (an inverted bowstring of 80-foot span), clearly shows the massive strengthening of 1926; a very deep central longitudinal, in steel, is inserted beneath, with stays beneath to the bowstring girders (earlier, in 1905, additional cross girders had been installed). *Harold D. Bowtell*

Below This is Crozier Holme (No 75, 101-foot skew) seen looking westward with an up train approaching. This view shows features of the strengthening of 1931, the transverse undergirders with outrigger extensions and stays (see overleaf). Note the superelevation of the curved road, and the longitudinal baulks beneath the rails. *Richard L. Pattinson/CRA*

less rigid stay wires to a tall signal post) were erected to give strength to the bowstrings.

Various extra vertical stays were also bolted on to the sides of the bowstring girders to improve rigidity. There was less interruption of railway traffic during this work than in carrying out the operation required for the inverted bowstring girder bridges.

These structures called for different treatment, as the lower curved flange was

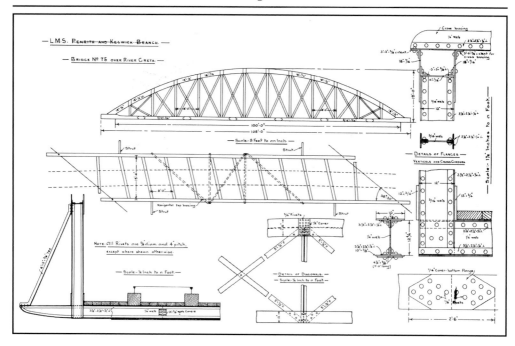

These Manchester (Hunts Bank) drawings of bridge No 75 show the structure in its original form, and as strengthened by the LMS. The later drawing (lower) is shown as 'drawn by C. A. Tysall, 29th Nov 1937', but the main work was done in 1931. The older drawing (upper) is believed to have been done by Jimmy Alexander, who had been third man at Barrow, Furness Railway, under Rutherford, the Chief Engineer (civil and mechanical) and Tom Mason, the second in command there. Mr Alexander went on to be District Engineer, Low Moor, after earlier promotion in Manchester. *Courtesy of Chief Civil Engineer, BR/LMR*

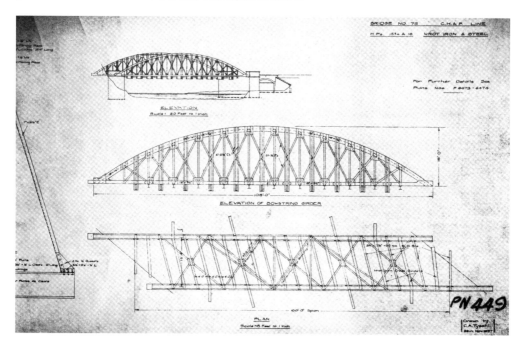

Brundholme, bridge No 71, an upright bowstring of 100-foot skew span, looking broadly east. Much strengthening is apparent in the sides, and beneath, while longitudinals are also riveted on top of the curved upper beams of the bowstrings. *Harold D. Bowtell*

overstressed in *tension* and the strength of the whole superstructure had to be increased. This was accomplished by installing a deep steel plate-web girder longitudinally beneath the centre of the bridge, the abutments being cut away to receive its ends. On completion, the new substantial under-girder carried a large share of the load of the bridge. Total occupation of the line and site was necessary during the crucial stages of the work on this type of bridge. An example readily viewed today is bridge No 59 at Stank Dub, Keswick.

The conversion to single track of the section between Blencow (exclusive) and Redhills Junction in mid-1938 enabled the stronger side of the underline bridges (none of which were major structures) to be retained and this was generally the up (original) side. This work completed the programme to give access as far as Keswick to locomotives such as Class '5MT' and '5X' 4-6-0s, although, until the new 60-foot turntable was commissioned at Keswick in the summer of 1939, it was not helpful to run these engines.

Some of the nominally lesser bridgeworks could have their problems. Roy Hughes has recalled from his early days as a bridge engineer, based at Hunt's Bank, Manchester, the replacement of Thornthwaite aqueduct, which carried the waters of a beck *over* the railway (a most unusual situation) to flow towards the Bassenthwaite Lake shore. There were two 'accommodation' farm lanes on the same bridge, above the water channel. The superstructure of the new bridge comprised a welded tank, fabricated in position on top of the old bridge, its weight being transferred to trestles from which it was lowered after the old bridge had been dismantled; the farm ways were replaced by a joint road on top of the covered aqueduct. During the operations the beck was diverted beside the railway into a large storage pond. At this critical stage torrential rain over-filled the stream and the railway became a river!

In this vicinity, sadly, the A66 road obliterates the course of the railway today together with part of the neighbouring meadows. However, a new bridge maintains the earlier tradition by carrying the aqueduct channel and providing access between the farms and their fields.

Rails Through Lakeland

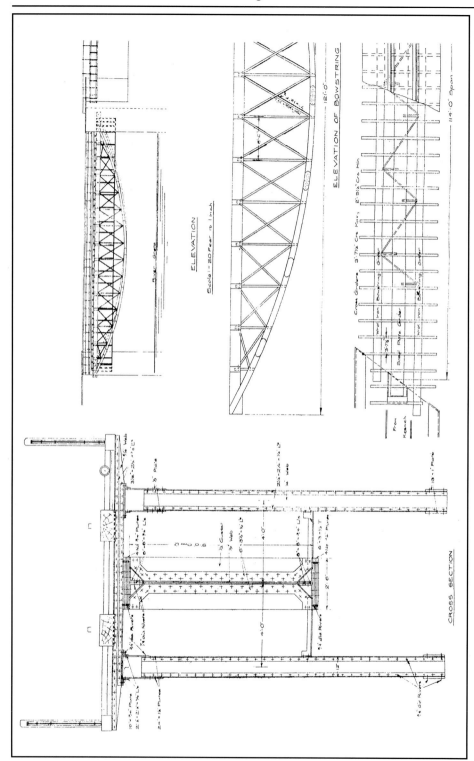

Part of the LMS drawing prepared for the strengthening of bridge 59 in 1933. The upper right portion of the drawing shows how the longitudinal girder lay between the bowstrings, while on the left is a vertical cross-section of the structure as modified. *J. M. Hammond Collection/Carlisle Record Office*

Bridge No 59, illustrated in detail on 4 April 1984, clearly showing the strengthening girder (see opposite). *Harold D. Bowtell*

Tragedy at Brigham, 16 December 1936

With one exception, the long-span bowstring girder bridges of the CKPR were left standing since the closure of the line and could still be studied in the late 1980s.

Another bridge of comparable design for long existed in the district of the C&WR line, and its construction was roughly contemporary with that of the CKPR's bridges. It was an upright bowstring girder structure, in wrought iron, crossing the River Derwent diagonally and carrying the single track of the M&CR Derwent branch from Bullgill to Brigham, opened in 1867 and giving M&CR trains access to Brigham, and thence to Cockermouth and Keswick. The span of 130 feet was greater than any of the CKPR line's bowstring girder bridges. The LMS closed the Derwent branch wef 29 April 1935 and towards the end of 1936 it put in hand the demolition of its most notable engineering feature, the bridge at Brigham.

The civil engineer in charge of the work was Richard Gauld, 40 years of age and highly regarded for his varied practical experience and professional knowledge. He was noted for his judgement and care, especially his concern

for men working with him. Mr Gauld had for several years been the LMS resident engineer, bridge gangs, in the Northern Division, based at the divisional headquarters, Hunt's Bank, Manchester; there were four gangs in the division. From August 1935 he held the appointment of resident engineer in charge of all LMS bridge gangs in England and Wales and was responsible to the Chief Engineer of the LMS.

Richard Gauld planned the method of dismantlement and entrusted it to his bridge gang based at Barrow. Work proceeded for some five weeks, with seven or eight men employed. On Wednesday 16 December 1936 the job was approaching a critical stage and Mr Gauld travelled from his home in Cheshire to take charge, arriving on site at 11.00am. The prevailing weather was typical of December in Cumberland, with the Derwent in spate and swift-flowing, but wind conditions did not call for postponement of the work. The deck of the bridge had been dismantled and steel cables had been secured and stretched across the river immediately beneath the bridge. This was in order to provide tension members when the oxy-

The LMS (originally M&CR) bridge (No 166) over the River Derwent at Brigham was dismantled during November-December 1936. This view shows the structure, looking north to the M&CR line, following closure (see the map on pages 26-7). This photograph was taken by Richard Gauld, the engineer, probably in the summer of 1936. *Albert Tims collection*

The same bridge in early December 1936, again recorded by Richard Gauld. The bridge has been prepared for demolition and partly dismantled. The temporary staying, in preparation for further weakening, is seen. Alexander Riddett (foreman) and Robert Hogg (inspector) are on the right.

The same scene on 18 December 1936, following the disaster of the 16th when Alexander Riddett and Richard Gauld were swept away to their deaths when the bridge collapsed into the swollen river. *R. L. Brydon*

acetylene cutting down of the bowstring side girders eliminated its upper curved boom (normally the compression member of the bridge) and converted the horizontal booms to compression members.

While the cutting operation was under way, there was suddenly a jerk when the crucial reversal of stress probably occurred (as visualised in advance) but the cables failed to play their part; one parted, and four men were hurled into the surging river below, clinging to scaffold planks. The men were Richard Gauld, Alexander ('Sandy') Riddett, foreman of the Barrow bridge gang, Robert Mitchell, chargehand plater and second man of the gang, and workman T. Davies. The alarm was conveyed by railway telephones from Brigham, westward to stations and signal boxes on the Workington line, which crossed and recrossed the Derwent in the next few miles. All within range of the emergency calls rushed to access points on the riverbanks, while at Camerton a barrier of wires and ropes was rigged across the river, secured to the structure of the footbridge that crossed the stream to reach the station. Davies was soon swirled into flooded fields on the left bank and was saved, although unconscious, by A. Birkett, station master at Broughton Cross. Robert Mitchell, a young man, succeeded in steering his plank towards the same bank and was successfully grabbed by Porter Weightman, also of Broughton Cross. Mitchell had been carried by the current, estimated at 15mph, close to Richard Gauld and almost propelled the latter's plank into arresting bushes on the bank. He thought he had achieved this but unhappily the engineer was carried on. Both Gauld and Riddett were seen, still clinging to their planks, further downstream, but the water was bitterly cold and both lost their lives.

A squall of wind may have contributed to the collapse, but the occurrence and its fatal outcome pointed, with hindsight, to the wisdom of a different or modified technique or equipment. More to the point, the job should perhaps have been postponed until a more favourable time of year. At least one friend and colleague of Richard Gauld held that the underlying cause was prevailing pressure on him to complete a heavy programme of work, of which this task was just one part, if a hazardous one. Another life could have been lost, but Mr Gauld had earlier noticed that his Inspector, Robert Hogg, was ill and had sent him home. Robert Mitchell reported that the engineer's last words, in the rushing stream, were of concern for Riddett, the Barrow foreman.

Subsequently, 22 colleagues contributed to a book entitled 'Richard Douglas Gauld, Civil Engineer: In Memoriam', in tribute to his kindness to his staff and friends. He was well known on the CKPR line and often motored out from Disley to be on site cheerfully through a wet Lakeland Sunday, to see a bridge job through to completion. On a lighter note, he was the engineer who, in charge of the reconstruction of bridge No 60 over Penrith Road, Keswick, in 1933, had problems because the steam crane was necessarily on the Penrith side of the bridge when its water ran low. It could not cross the gap to reach the water column – the 'elephant' – at Keswick station, so he organised the spectators into a human chain, from river to crane, passing buckets of water from one to another. Readers may recall a similar occurrence in the 1950s Ealing comedy *The Titfield Thunderbolt*! It perhaps illustrates the point that there can be a prototype for most things in the railway film and model world!

The reason for the reconstruction of bridge No 60 was to enable it to carry the 36-ton steam crane that would uphold the east end of the new plate-web girder to be added to the adjacent bridge No 59.

4. The permanent way

The C&WR permanent way

In the period 1856-60 (at least), sleepers were being ordered from Mr McGlasson; the price in 1860 was 3s 8d each for sleepers 10 inches wide, 5 inches deep and 9 feet long. This railway's independent existence was during the time of iron rails and, ten years after its opening, the C&WR was still ordering rails of the early 'bridge' section, which had a broad base, or legs, bolted down to sleepers, and a narrower head or running surface. These rails weighed 72lb per yard and were punched ready to take the holding-down bolts; they were invoiced at £8 15s 0d per ton, at Gateshead. After mid-1866 the C&WR was integrated with the LNWR and the practices of that company's Lancaster & Carlisle section prevailed, as explained later.

The CKPR permanent way

This company also employed iron rails in its early years. Its first orders were placed in the years 1861-62, in anticipation of the contractor's progress with the works; the Aberdare Company were to supply the rails, Cowan & Sheldon of Carlisle the chairs and Hopkins & Company of Middlesbrough the fishplates, bolts and nuts. Thus, chaired rail was preferred to the earlier pattern bridge rail. When the track was mostly laid and opening of the line in prospect, the Board of Trade required (July 1864) that all the chairs adjoining rail joints should be replaced by heavier items, around a month's work. By the end of September 1864 the BOT was content with the track, although fringe problems remained.

Replacement with steel rails commenced early in 1871, after some six years of operating on the iron road, and the main programme of renewals was completed during the years 1871-75, when 2,700 tons of new steel rails of (mostly) 76lb per yard section were acquired – from Barrow Hematite Steel Company in 1871-72, but from West Cumberland Iron & Steel Company, of Workington, in 1874-75. The price paid was £11 per ton in March 1871, rising steeply to £15 per ton in August 1872, then falling back to £10 per ton in October 1874 and progressively to £9 1s 3d per ton (for a substantial order of 1,000 tons) by December 1875. Some iron rails remained in use, but doubtless in sidings, until a special effort was made to clear them, in 1879-82. A scrap sale price of £3 to £3 10s per ton was the general order and a dealer in Middlesbrough, who quoted £6s 6d 0d per ton in February 1880, not surprisingly found that he had overreached himself and cancelled his order in May.

Also in 1880 it was reported by CKPR Engineer John Wood that the company had until then used larch sleepers, with chairs of 20lb weight, and heavier chairs of 30lb weight adjoining rail joints, this feature no doubt deriving from the BOT's stipulation of 1864. He further reported that no accidents had resulted in the course of 15 years running, but it was noted that the LNWR (L&C section) had latterly substituted chairs of 46lb in its road. It was therefore agreed to use heavier chairs and imported (and creosoted) sleepers in future for progressive replacements.

The price of steel rails fell remarkably after the boom of the earlier 1880s. Supplies in 1885 came from the West Cumberland Iron & Steel Co Ltd at £5 per ton, and in 1888 from Charles Cammell & Company (the most recently established of West Cumberland steelmasters) at only £3 19s 0d

A vintage view of a group of permanent way staff seen by their cabin, in a westward view towards Bassenthwaite Lake station. *Richard L. Pattinson/CRA*

per ton, delivered from Workington to Cockermouth; this was the cheapest of three competitive quotations. Rails of 1892, ordered for doubling a section of the CKPR route, cost about £4 10s 0d per ton.

Rail sections were reviewed by the CKPR towards the end of 1897, it being noted that the Caledonian Railway had adopted 90lb per yard for relaying its main lines, while the NBR employed 92lb per yard; be it noted that this was a time when much heavier locomotives were coming into service on the northern lines. The CKPR adopted 84lb per yard and abandoned the use of a double-headed (reversible) section. Both Cammells, of Derwent Works, and Moss Bay Iron & Steel Company, of Moss Bay Works, quoted £4 12s 6d per ton for 84lb per yard rails in February 1898; in the event Cammells' quotation was accepted. Rails for widening works were supplied in 1900 by both Cammells and Moss Bay at £7 7s 6d to £7 12s 6d per ton, but delivered to Troutbeck and Blencow. Similar rails were being acquired in 1909 at

£5 18s 6d (after some haggling and reduction in price) from Moss Bay Hematite Iron & Steel Co Ltd. The amalgamated Workington Iron & Steel Co Ltd (James V. Ellis, Commercial and General Manager) quoted in January 1912 for steel rails 'to Mr Sandberg's latest specification for silicon steel' at 85lb per yard, to British Standard (BS) section; an order for 260 tons was placed in August 1913, at £6 1s 3d per ton, for delivery over a period. Following the review of line and structures by Mr Thurstan of the LNWR in 1913, significant relaying was required and the cost was kept down by purchase of enough second-hand materials from the LNWR's 'Marron line' (the 'Joint line', presumably) to relay 4 miles of CKPR track with 27-30-foot rail lengths at 80lb and upward per yard. Wartime supplies were not always available, and by February 1916 85lb per yard BS rails were quoted at £10 17s 6d per ton. The state of the main line and passing places in June 1916 was recorded as follows:

LNWR 'Special DX' 0-6-0 No 1424 works a ballast train at Keswick some time between 1890 and 1910, and before the background trees grew up. *Stanley J. Rhodes collection*

Total mileage	41 miles 30 chains
Comprising:	
84lb rails of 1898 onward	17miles 60 chains
85lb rails of 1913	
and 1916	3 miles 2 chains
80lb rails of 1914	
and 1916	4 miles 44 chains
76lb rails of 1888-95	9 miles 40 chains
76lb rails of 1872-76	6 miles 44 chains

Doubling of the CKPR line

As we have already seen, the provision of a second track between Derwent Junction (Workington) and Cockermouth Junction was achieved piecemeal between about 1857 and completion in 1868. The CKPR was built as a single track route throughout, apart from provision to cross trains at (initially) four of the intermediate stations. The need for double track became apparent as traffic developed in the 1880s and 1890s, especially over the steep gradients between Keswick and Penrith, notably between Threlkeld and Troutbeck. In December 1892 the Permanent Way Committee reviewed the situation and recorded that Threlkeld to Troutbeck was a section of 4 miles 59 chains and had always

been difficult to work, as the line climbed eastward from Threlkeld station for about three-quarters of a mile at 1 in 68, then at 1 in 62 for the whole distance beyond. The times usually taken by trains to traverse the section were:

	Passenger	General goods	Minerals
Down			
(westbound)	10min	13min	15min
Up			
(eastbound)	14min	18-20min	20min

However, due to weather and other factors, the eastbound times ranged to 30 minutes, and even 40 minutes when normal loads were exceeded. The normal service of the previous summer had reached 16 trains daily in each direction, comprising eight passenger, four mineral, three goods services and one ballast train. To these were added on most days relief or special excursion passenger trains and some additional goods trains, the additions sometimes numbering six or eight in the day, with the heavy long-distance

The track is probably viewed here in LMS times, but the warning board addressed to train crews about to descend the bank dates from CKPR days. *Richard L. Pattinson/CRA*

excursions arriving, westbound to Keswick, during the morning and leaving, eastbound up the gradient, towards evening. These heavy excursions sometimes had to be shunted from one line to the other at Troutbeck (or elsewhere) to permit other traffic to overtake. As long as the up traffic was worked under 'permissive block', three or four trains had been allowed to follow one another on the 4¼ miles of ascent. However, by recent Board of Trade order an intermediate block post had been built at Highgate and not more than two trains could now be accommodated at one time between Threlkeld and Troutbeck. As land for doubling had nearly all been purchased under Board authority of December 1891, the committee recommended execution of the work of doubling this section of line.

R. H. Hodgson secured the contract for the formation work, presumed to include bridges (there were two underline viaducts to widen), while the supply and laying of track was undertaken by the railway company. Work was in hand from around July 1893 and was generally complete, with provisional approval granted by the Board of Trade in August 1894, formal approval being secured in December of

that year. The company obtained an Act of 1 June 1894 in order to regularise the financing of the widening works.

The next step was the doubling east of Troutbeck. No attempt was made to widen between Penruddock and Blencow, a section with an underline viaduct and heavy earthworks, including a rock cutting. Neither was widening contemplated between Redhills Junction and Penrith No 1 signal box, a portion of the route not traversed by the majority of mineral trains or long-distance passenger excursion trains. However, in March 1900 contracts were placed with W. Grisenthwaite of Penrith, for the formation on two sections: Section 1 was from Redhills Junction to Blencow, at a tender price of £4,820 11s 3d; and Section 2 was from Troutbeck to Penruddock, the tender price being £5203 19s 6d.

Mr Grisenthwaite had optimistically undertaken to complete his work by 16 September 1900 – a mere six months – and the company was displeased when their inspections between October 1900 and January 1901 revealed that progress was well behind target. The double line from Troutbeck to Penruddock was eventually

At the east end of Keswick station, Jack Tyson (left) is ganger in charge of the Keswick 'length'; Jack Mills (centre) and Jack Ward are members, in LMS days. *Jack Tyson collection*

brought into use on 1 June 1901, with Board of Trade authority and subject to the recommendations of Colonel Yorke being complied with. By 8 August 1901 the Board of Trade had provided a copy of Major Druitt's report on both newly doubled sections of line and it is believed that both were in use.

Reconversion of sections to single track is covered in the chapters dealing with stations and signalling of the route in LMS and BR days.

5. Signalling and gas lighting

Signalling on the C&WR

The term 'signalling' must have had a very limited meaning for the C&WR's 9 miles of route. After ten years of existence, in March 1857, the company agreed to contribute to the Whitehaven Junction Railway's expenditure on installation of semaphore signals in the areas of Workington joint station yard and Derwent Junction. In April 1861 the C&WR itself instructed the Electric Telegraph Company to install a single telegraph line between Workington and Cockermouth, with three single-needle transmitting instruments, at a rental of £55 a year.

In May 1865, nearing the end of its days, the C&WR became concerned at the total absence of distant (warning) signals for its 'roadside stations', so Saxby & Farmer was commissioned to supply and erect semaphore signals at all those locations at a cost of £506 15s 6d. A year or so later the railway was part of the LNWR and its more critical approach and practices towards signalling began to take effect.

Signalling on the CKPR

The CKPR itself was little more than 30 miles in length but it came on the scene at a time when railway companies throughout Britain, and the Board of Trade as their 'keeper', were beginning to evolve and encourage more sophisticated systems for safer operation. This called for better communications, the provision of semaphore signals and associated equipment and buildings – and more men.

The Board of the CKPR company turned down an early suggestion from the LNWR that it might at the start secure adequate land to permit later doubling of its line. All bridgeworks and other structures, with formation and main running lines, were thus designed for a single track, with loops to permit 'crossing' of up and down trains initially at Cockermouth (passenger station), Bassenthwaite Lake, Keswick and Penruddock stations. Troutbeck, between Keswick and Penruddock, was provided with a crossing loop in 1874, nine years after the general opening to traffic.

The suggestion that electric telegraph communication would assist safer dispatch of traffic on the railway came in October 1862 from contractors George Boulton & Sons, who were by then at work on construction. The telegraph was installed between Penrith and Keswick – and subsequently also between Keswick and Cockermouth. In due course the LNWR's well-tried telegraph regulations provided a model for the CKPR. A few years after the opening of the line it was noted that station masters on the CKPR must be able to read and use telegraph communication – 'on pain of dismissal'.

The Telegraph Acts of 1868 and 1869 nationalised the services in Britain and the telegraph company handed over the Penrith-Cockermouth installation to the Postmaster General, who paid the CKPR £1,300; the railway company thenceforward provided and operated the relevant lines with, in general, priority for their needs over the PMG's public messages. Progressively, telegraph messages lost their relevance for safe working of a railway but they long retained importance for the railway's commercial communications, even into the 1950s and early 1960s.

The 'train staff' method of working the CKPR was in force from the start of public operation in January 1865, and the Board of

Trade had been appraised of the details. A substantial wooden 'staff' was allocated to the section between each pair of 'staff stations' and represented the authority for a locomotive driver to travel over the route between the specified pair of stations. He was forbidden to run over the section concerned without the staff in his possession.

Block telegraph working, with its purposely designed and distinctive instruments, is something that one has come to relate to double-track railways rather than single lines, but in 1869 the Board of Trade (in accordance with its contemporary views) recommended it to the CKPR. The Keswick Board, not enamoured of the complication and expense envisaged, instructed its Secretary to reply, detailing reasons for not adopting it on the Lakeland line. By November 1874, following a fatal collision between passenger trains near Norwich, the Board of Trade pressed the matter and this time the Keswick company acted promptly and installed the block telegraph. It was used solely to control the passage of trains and provided a means of securing authority to pass a train from one station or other 'block post' to the next; even so, the appropriate staff was still handed out to the driver as tangible evidence of his authority to enter a single-line section. It is interesting that in the LNWR's record of single lines and train staff sections throughout its widely dispersed spheres of operation, in 1885 only one section of one route had the benefit of a train tablet system, or equivalent, and that appears below:

From LNWR Appendix, April 1885
Single Lines and Train Staff Sections, West Cumberland Division, CK&P Line Section:
Train Staffs:
Cockermouth Junc and Cockermouth*

Cockermouth and Bassenthwaite Lake	Round Yellow
Bassenthwaite Lake and Keswick	Round Red
Keswick and Troutbeck	Round Blue
Troutbeck and Penruddock	Round Yellow
Penruddock and Redhills Junction	Round Red
Redhills Junction and Penrith	Round White

*Tyer's Train Tablet System was in operation between Cockermouth Junction and Cockermouth station.

Block telegraph was also operational in addition throughout.

It may be noted that Embleton, Braithwaite, Threlkeld and Blencow had not achieved the status of train staff stations at the time of this LNWR Appendix and that only one focal point for train staffs at Keswick is implied; this may have been either the old westerly signal box or the station master's office. Staff working was supplemented at discretion by 'staff and ticket' working, reinforced by the block system, and successive trains could be despatched from one block post to another by giving each driver a ticket (of authority), while also showing him the relevant staff, until arrival of the last driver of the sequence, who would be given the staff to carry through the section.

Reverting to the 1870s, CKPR Engineer John Wood reported in October 1873 from his formal professional address at the time, at 8 Victoria Chambers, Westminster, on the current disposition of points and signals on the railway. As was common among railways of the period, the basic signalling at a typical crossing station consisted of a platform signal, sited near the station master's office (which contained the Post Office telegraph instruments and housed a train staff for each section, when the staff was not out in use). A semaphore arm for each direction of travel was displayed on the post of the platform signal and a distant signal for each direction of travel was sited some distance out. Most of the main-line facing points were bolt locked with the distant signals, but not at Cockermouth, where both up and down trains used the platform nearest the town. Mr Wood was thereupon authorised to remodel the signalling at Cockermouth, Bassenthwaite Lake, Keswick, Troutbeck and Penruddock stations at a cost quoted by the chosen signalling contractors, Saxby & Farmer, of about £3,500. Signals would be erected to

Above Various signal boxes figure in the 'landscape' views already presented, so in this chapter interiors and unusual aspects are illustrated in greater detail. This first photograph shows Cockermouth station signal box, which started life as a Saxby & Farmer installation of 1875, part of the CKPR's first 'modern' signalling to meet Board of Trade demands. It is seen after the LMS had installed a replacement MR-style lever frame, facing south, away from the main running lines, which are in the foreground. *David Jenkinson*

Below Keswick No 2 box ('Box A' until 1924) originally contained a Saxby & Farmer lever frame of 1874 and the structure was also of that company's architecture. The building suffered modification in time, and during the 1930s a LNWR frame was installed, facing (unusually) towards the rear of the cabin. The range of workshops behind the cabin also dated from CKPR times. *David Jenkinson*

Penruddock signal box was of CKPR design and construction in 1896, with a Tweedy frame. It replaced a Saxby installation of 1874. A special train for Keswick Convention is seen on 15 July 1967. *Derek Cross*

Mr Tyer, pioneer signal engineer, put in for the CKPR his successive designs of train tablet instruments for working single lines, and the last variant was the 'Tyers No 6'. This example is illustrated in the workshops, but for many years the type was found in CKPR signal boxes and station offices. On authorisation received electrically from the box in advance, the signalman could pull out the drawer at the bottom of the case and remove a circular brass tablet as authority for the engine driver to proceed through the section. This tablet had engraved upon it the name of the relevant track section and it was the driver's duty to check that he has received the correct tablet. He gave it up on reaching the next box. *Harold D. Bowtell, courtesy of Gordon Nichol*

meet the Board of Trade's standards: basically comprising distant, home and starting signals for each direction for a simple crossing station on the single line. All facing points would have facing point locks, which, along with other points on main running lines and the semaphore signals, would be worked from a signal box, housing a fully interlocked lever frame, under the direct control of a signalman. The work was completed progressively by December 1875; in the process, Cockermouth was provided with independent up and down platform lines for through passenger trains and

Troutbeck became a crossing station, with both up and down platforms.

Another unique feature of the table of staff sections in 1885 was the reference to the Tyer's train tablet system, in force between Cockermouth Junction and Cockermouth station. It put the CKPR well ahead of its time. Mr Tyer had recently inaugurated his invention on the Callander & Oban line, operated by the Caledonian Railway, when early in 1883 he wrote to further prospective clients, including the CKPR. The neighbouring M&CR showed a cheeky initiative in writing to Keswick to request that the Tyer's tablet system be introduced on the single track from the Junction to the passenger station at Cockermouth 'to obviate the repeated delays' – presumably referring to delays to the M&CR's modest local passenger trains from Bullgill (on its Carlisle line) via Linefoot and Brigham, to Cockermouth. The CKPR was interested in this proposal and by

August 1883 approval by the Board of Trade and the LNWR was obtained and a year's trial was authorised. The equipment was installed and had operated successfully for nearly five years when a review was undertaken. As a result Mr Tyer's improved (No 2 or 2A) type of electric tablet instruments were installed during 1889 at Cockermouth station (one instrument – presumably supplementing the existing installation), Bassenthwaite Lake (two) and Keswick (one), followed c1891 by comparable instruments at Keswick (one – additional to the 1889 installation), Troutbeck (two), Penruddock (two), Redhills (two) and Penrith (one) – while leaving existing block instruments in the 'intermediate or non-passing stations'.

There remained one creaking skeleton in the CKPR's signalling cupboard. When the Secretary and the Engineer of the company met General Hutchinson of the Board of Trade on 18 June 1892, to consider primarily

The LMS quickly replaced all Tyers tablet instruments on the CKPR with Tyers 'key token' equipment. This pair are illustrated in the station office at Embleton; one is concerned with working to/from Cockermouth and the other is for the opposite direction, to/from Bassenthwaite Lake; in the latter section, the 'key' was used to release the ground frame for access to Close Quarry sidings. *Phoebe Wallace, courtesy of Thompson collection*

A group of Tyers' key tokens used in the instruments at Embleton and neighbouring cabins. They are inscribed (L-R): Braithwaite-Bassenthwaite Lake; Bassenthwaite Lake-Embleton; Embleton-Cockermouth Station; Brigham-Cockermouth. *Harold D. Bowtell, courtesy of Gordon Nichol*

the relatively innocuous topic of signal arrangements at the small or non-passing stations, the General's attention became sharply focused on the revelation that permissive block working (trains following one another at sight or time interval) was operated between Threlkeld and Troutbeck in the up (eastbound) direction for some 4¼ miles, mostly ascending at the tough inclination of 1 in 62. An ultimatum was delivered: three months were allowed to bring in absolute block working on this portion of line. The problem had come about through pressure of traffic, especially slow-moving empty coke trains from the West Cumberland furnaces to Durham collieries, and the succession of return excursion trains running from Keswick to mainly NER destinations. The CKPR management had already been aware of its predicament, and had been buying land for widening the line and making the necessary plans, so they brought forward the establishment of a small intermediate block post (signal box) at Highgate and thereafter the doubling of the whole section from a rebuilt station at Threlkeld to Troutbeck, and eventually also from Troutbeck to Penruddock and between Blencow and Redhills Junction.

The CKPR engineer was responsible, in the 1865-1922 period, for signalling as well as civil engineering, permanent way and buildings. While his main needs (including the earliest signal boxes) were designed and

The unique little signal cabin of 1892 at Highgate was, from 1894, upgraded as a block post on the double line and thereafter housed a Tweedy frame of four levers. This view is eastward, in May 1983; the 'hump' beyond the box is the remains of the down platform used by schoolchildren from 1908 to 1928. *Harold D. Bowtell*

This 'snapshot' of May 1931 records the end of Willie Nicholson's service as signalman at Highgate, in the month when the block post was abandoned as an LMS economy and Mr Nicholson and family had to move away to, eventually, Carnforth. *Elizabeth Cook, courtesy of Mrs Elizabeth Cook*

usually supplied by signalling contractors, notably Saxby & Farmer and Tyer, he later built boxes of distinctive designs, also making and modifying equipment and semaphore signals. The workshop accommodation for his fitters at Keswick was very restricted. The company's blacksmith had other work to do and it is recalled that local smiths were called on from time to time to work on signal locking frames, and probably also in making rods, cranks and other components.

Signal boxes and junctions on the route

The following table sets out the signal boxes on the route of the line from Derwent Junction (Workington) to Cockermouth Junction (opened in 1847 but only tabulated in its double-track form), and on the CKPR from Cockermouth Junction to Penrith No 1 signal box (opened to passengers in 1865). It touches on the main changes that affected signalling at each site, through both expansion and subsequent decline and closure of the route, ending effectively with the introduction of electric working on the West Coast Main Line between Preston to Glasgow, when BR's newly electrified Anglo-Scottish expresses swept for the first time past the site of Penrith No 1 box and the obliterated junction with the CKPR, in May 1974.

Signal boxes (and subsidiary signalling frames) between Derwent Junction (Workington) and Penrith (No 1)

Mileages shown are as recorded by the LNWR in 1906. As was commonplace in LNWR/LMS practice, distances varied a little over the years, even when the structures remained firmly unmoved!

Miles/ yards	Name Type and date	History and remarks	Closure date
-	Derwent Junction Saxby, probably c1870	Replaced a pointsman's cabin of 1847. Box had oversight of ground frame (GF) for Merchants Quay branch divergence. LNWR locking frame installed 1888. Box replaced by BR in 1955 with 1943-type frame of 40 levers.	1955 box replaced by GF on 12-13.11.1988
-/1,436	Workington Bridge Junction LNWR type, 1885	There was a hint in 1877 of the building (impending?) of this box.	c1950
-/568	Derwent Tin Plate Works Sidings 1872	Beer Pot Siding and Bear Pot Gate dated from 1847. Box ceased to be a block post c1910; shown on plan, 1915. Barepot level crossing (LC) just to the east survived.	Box probably demolished 1916-22. Closed 18.4.1966
-	Seaton Mill LC 1847	Never a block post; for many years under oversight of William Pit box.	18.4.1966
1/37	William Pit Colliery (becoming William Pit Sidings) LNWR type, 1881	Contained LNWR frame of 14 (later 18) levers.	27.1.1965
-/1,248	Camerton Probably 1870s	Replaced a pointsman of 1847. Open only as required by 1906. Ceased to be a block post by 1916. Replaced from 20.6.1935 by open GF (2 levers) entitled 'Camerton Station Level Crossing', but sited at colliery junction east of old box.	Box and frame survived to 1935. 27.1.1965 (GF)

Miles/ yards	Name Type and date	History and remarks	Closure date
1/499	Marron Junction LNWR type, 1902	Replaced West and East boxes of c1871 (Nos 1 & 2?) which had themselves replaced pointsman's cabins. Box replaced by GF (2 levers) from 7.11.1960. In 1847 pointsman required at Broughton Cross but GF at that station was never a signal box or block post.	Probably 26.1.1965 (GF)
1/1,704	Brigham No 2 LNWR type, 1883	Site enjoyed some supervision 1847-1966 because of LC at west end of station. Another signal box shown on map of 1898 to westward, on down side, at junction for quarries branch, but by 1905 reference is to GF (although 'signal box' survived here on diagram of 1915). GF of one lever remained in 1950s.	See below
-/196	Brigham No 1 LNWR type, 1877	Control in some form at this site would date from 1867, when M&CR branch to Bullgill opened.	See below
	Brigham LMS, c1933	Replaced Nos 2 and 1 boxes in 1936. Sited at west end of station but east of LC. Contained LMS reversed frame of 29 (later 30) levers. Operation eastward became single 16.5.1960.	18.4.1966
1/1,430	Cockermouth Junction Built 1864 and 1873-76. LNWR type, 1886. GF installed 1960	Running Junction opened from C&WR (soon to be LNWR) to newly built CKPR late 1864. First true signal box built on down side at this period. Responsibility of CKPR 1864-1922. Electric tablet working to station from 1883. Replaced by new box on up side 1886; LNWR frame of 27 (later 36) levers.	16.5.1960 (box); 29.9.1965 (GF)
	Cockermouth Gas Works LNWR-type GF, 1920s	Never a block post. GF had 2 levers, released by key token for section.	1963
-/924	Cockermouth Station Saxby, 1875	Saxby frame of 40 levers. Box structure modified over the years. Replacement LMS 45-lever frame of 1941 (or 1935?) installed, reversed to face south (as was the earlier one?).	18.4.1966
2/1,364	Embleton (never a box here)	Open GFs installed for yard and by LC. Block instruments in station, replaced c1893 by electric tablet instruments.	18.4.1966
-	Rakefoot LC (no box) 1864	Never a block post. Acquired LNWR GF but later signals were connected by wire to gates.	18.4.1966
-	Close Granite Quarry Sidings (no box) 1912	Never a block post. LNWR-type GF dated 1912 put in by CKPR. Released by tablet for section.	1953 or 1954

Miles/ yards	Name Type and date	History and remarks	Closure date
2/550	Bassenthwaite Lake Saxby, 1874	Replaced by CKPR box 1911, with Tweedy frame. Electric tablet working in each direction from 1889. Additional small crude 2-lever box put in at east end by CKPR, 1902	18.4.1966 (both boxes)
4/1,694	Braithwaite (never a box here)	Open GFs installed for yard and by LC. Block instruments in station office, replaced c1893 by electric tablet instruments (akin to Embleton).	18.4.1966
2/792	Keswick Box 'A' (Keswick No 2 from c1924) Saxby, 1874	Original Saxby frame replaced in existing box c1931 by LNWR type with 24 (later 25) levers reversed in back of box – unusual practice for LNWR frame.	Ceased to be block post wef 18.4.1966 when line westward closed. 4.12.1967
-	Keswick Box 'B' (Keswick No 1 from c1924) CKPR, probably 1889	Located on south end of down platform. Replaced by LMS box with reversed LMS frame of 24 levers in 1932.	4.12.1967
-	Briery Siding GF (no box) 1892	Never a block post. Open Tweedy GF (2 levers) released by tablet for section. Not used commercially after 1958.	Removed c1962
3/836	Threlkeld CKPR, 1893	Tweedy 18-lever frame retained throughout. Electric tablet working with Keswick and Troutbeck introduced probably 1892, ie before box commissioned. Authority to cross trains given by BOT 'recently' (as at 4.10.1893); authority for double-line working eastward given 8.1894.	4.12.1967
2/880	Highgate CKPR, 1892	Internal Tweedy 4-lever frame, but not installed and in use until c8-10.1894. Block post on single line from 9.11.1892; double line from August 1894.	5.1931
2/418	Troutbeck Saxby, 1874	Saxby frame. Became block post and crossing place on single line from date of box. Electric tablet working with Threlkeld introduced probably 1892 (but note that Highgate was opened late 1892) and with Penruddock likewise. Double-line block working with Highgate from 8.1894, and with Penruddock from 6.1901 or 7.1901. Seemingly after 1901 – date unknown – replacement 16-lever Tweedy frame installed. In later years the box could switch out.	21.11.1966 or 5.12.1966?
2/462	Penruddock Saxby, 1874	Saxby frame. Located at down end of up platform. Was crossing place from the start in 1865, with train staff. Staff working with Troutbeck and Redhills Junction from 1874. Electric tablet working with both those boxes from probably 1892. Double-line block with Troutbeck from 6.1901 or 7.1901, but	4.12.1967

Miles/ yards	Name Type and date	History and remarks	Closure date
		working eastward always single line (tablet to Blencow from 1901). Replacement CKPR box at up end of up platform with 18-lever Tweedy frame dated from 1896. Instruments removed from box to station office in LMS days (or a little later). Small supplementary box at west end of layout existed only 1896-1901 (until doubling).	
⁀	Harrison's Lime Works siding (Flusco) (no box) 1916	Never a block post. Original GF probably by Tweedy. Replaced 1938 by 2-lever Tweedy frame released by key token for section.	19.6.1972
⁀	Flusco Quarry Siding (no box) 1892	Never a block post. GF released by tablet for section.	c1922
4/22	Blencow CKPR, 1901	22-lever Tweedy frame, replaced 1938 by 35-lever LMS frame reversed in back of box. Electric token (Tyer's tablets in CKPR days, as elsewhere) working with Penruddock from opening of box in 1901. Note that Blencow station was not a crossing place prior to coming of box and double-line block working with Redhills Junction box, 6.1901-17.6.1938, after which single-line electric token working (with key tokens, LMS practice) applied between Blencow and Penrith No 1. (GF in use for Blencowe Quarry connection at Blencow station 4.12.1967 until final closure of line wef 19.6.1972.)	4.12.1967
2/110	Redhills Junction Believed NER, 1866	Replaced by CKPR brick box of c1890, with Tweedy frame, having air of earlier Saxby-type structure. Note single-line electric tablet working with Penruddock and Penrith No 1 from probably 1892, but NER/LNER link with Eamont Junction box (originally an LNWR box, 1866) was always double track. On CKPR double-line block with Blencow in 6.1901, when that box opened with section of double track.	17.6.1938
1/418	Penrith No 1 (Keswick Junction) LNWR type, 1879-80	Main-line box replacing earlier cabins (see Volume 1, pp118-121). Note that Keswick line's final portion, Flusco-Blencow-Penrith, closed wef 19.6.1972	5.3.1973

Redhills Junction signal box and signalman. Note that the nameboard is akin to that on the earlier 'snap' of Highgate. *Richard L. Pattinson/CRA*

Approaching Bassenthwaite Lake station, eastbound, a two-car 'Derby lightweight' DMU is nearing the up platform. The CKPR made a pretty job architecturally when replacing the Saxby cabin here with this example of its own design, placed marginally closer to the level crossing, in 1911. A rather crude little subsidiary cabin containing a ground frame was sited at the opposite end of the station for working the points at the far end of the lengthy crossing loop. *National Railway Museum, York*

The lever frame in the 1911 Bassenthwaite Lake signal box was by Tweedy of Carlisle. Edwin Thompson is seen as signalman, c1964. *Phoebe Wallace, courtesy of Thompson collection*

Left On the main down platform at Keswick, the unusual construction of CKPR signal box 'B' is apparent – and we also have a glimpse of the signalman and his lever frame. The LMS renamed this box 'Keswick No 1' and replaced it in 1932. *J. W. Brownrigg* collection

Below left A sunny day at Keswick during the later 1950s finds a 'Derby lightweight' DMU coasting into the main down platform at Keswick, bound for Workington. The driver is holding out the leather-covered hoop and pouch for collection by the signalman from the replacement 1932 box. The pouch contains the token that has authorised the driver to work over the single-line section from Threlkeld. *Ivor Nicholas*

Above Threlkeld box always housed a Tweedy frame of 18 levers, of 1893. The layout diagram is seen and Bob Wren is 'pulling off' for the up road, probably c1966. *Phoebe Wallace, courtesy of Jack Tyson collection*

Below The signalling arrangements at Threlkeld from 1893-94, as drawn by LNWR signalling chronicler and historian Richard Foster.

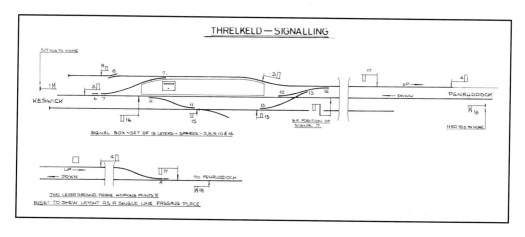

The approach to Keswick from the west: the LNWR bracket signal, which presumably replaced a CKPR signal in LMS days, is well loaded with balance weights, and 'slotted', to permit shared operation with No 2 box (glimpsed over the ballast wagon) and the quite distant No 1 box. *Richard L. Pattinson/CRA*

Contrasting with the LNWR bracket signal at Keswick, this is the up home marking the end of the single line approaching Blencow; both signal and box are of CKPR origin. Observe the alternative route by the up goods loop, left. *Richard L. Pattinson/CRA*

The approach to Keswick station from the east also featured an LNWR home signal, slotted for shared operation, but its configuration as seen is unusual. The road is set for a down train to enter the outer face of the up island platform. The signal box on the down platform was built by the LMS c1932. *Richard L. Pattinson/CRA*

Above A general view of the LMS signal box at Brigham, built in 1933. *Peter W. Robinson*

Below An interior view at Brigham. The LNWR normally placed signal box lever frames so that the signalman faced the line while operating his points and signals and could keep a continuous watch on trains and other movements. This interior at Brigham illustrates the LMS company's adoption of frames based on Midland Railway practice and installed 'back to front'. Joseph Watson is working the level crossing gates. The loading bank and limestone sidings can be glimpsed to the west, over the crossing. *Phoebe Wallace*

Lighting by acetylene gas

The CKPR used the town's gas for lighting Cockermouth Joint station, probably from its opening, and there was a public electricity supply to Keswick station and yard from 1899-1900 onwards. Most railways used paraffin oil lamps at lesser stations, as also for signal lamps. Remarkably, the wayside stations on the CKPR acquired individual gas generators, which have been described as looking like an old-fashioned washing boiler in a wash-house, which was in fact the 'gas house'. Water was fed by gravity to acetylene (housed in a container that was recharged daily) and the reaction produced gas, which was then piped to the various lamps. These embraced external lights on platforms, yards and approaches, as well as in rooms and in various neighbouring signals.

The following dates are those of authorisation, which was followed by an order to the manufacturers of the equipment. Penruddock came first (November 1898), and a larger-capacity plant was soon substituted

The ground frame at Limestone Sidings, Brigham, was released by an Annetts key, normally held in the signal box and here seen with its lettering 'Brigham'. *Harold D. Bowtell, courtesy of Gordon Nichol*

Here is a gas generating plant, disused but virtually complete, seen in 1985 in the 'gas house' at Threlkeld station. The two horizontal lower circular chambers held the charges of carbide. Water could be admitted via one or other downpipe, to the selected charge. Gas was then generated until exhaustion of the carbide, when the top cock could be switched over to divert the water to the unused charge. The duty porter would recharge the plant as required. As gas was produced it would rise into the cylindrical vertical holder (the upper section of which, seen on the left, fitted tight on top). The gas filter is to the right, on the piping to the station lamps, and those in the railway houses. *Harold D. Bowtell*

The gas house is visible in this view of Threlkeld: it is the building on the banking between the up line and the stationmaster's house, beyond the signal. The fireman of the 'Mickey Mouse' 2-6-0 is enjoying the ride downgrade as his train rolls into the station, westbound. The distinctive signal box is glimpsed at the far end of the island platform buildings. *Preston Whiteley*

(August 1899). Then came Blencow, which received Penruddock's original plant (in August 1899) but which was subsequently fitted with a larger replacement plant (in August 1901). There followed Braithwaite and Threlkeld (both in April 1902), but the Threlkeld plant was a large one, providing for 50 lamps, and its replacement (in August 1916) was for 40 lamps. At Troutbeck (December 1903) the plant went back to a standard capacity, like the replacement installations at Penruddock and Blencow, but was probably enlarged in 1910. Bassenthwaite Lake was authorised in June 1907. Finally, Embleton (December 1909) was to have a plant with the modest capacity of 20 lamps; this equipment, including lamps, piping and installation, as well as its shed, cost £49 10s 0d from John Lee & Company, of Hull. A replacement gas house was proposed at Embleton in 1949 and certainly a plant

operated here until after closure of the station to public use, and into the early 1960s.

From a date in the 1950s or early 1960s, as the gas equipment became worn out, replacement paraffin oil lamps were installed, sometimes preceded by a temporary interlude with Tilley pressure lamps. Some stations still had gas lamps until closure in 1966 (west of Keswick) or the loss of their staff in 1968 (east of Keswick).

An amusing characteristic of the acetylene equipment was the fading of the lights on frosty nights. When this occurred, the station master had to hasten out from his cosy house bearing a kettle of boiling water with which to thaw the freezing water in the supply tank within the gas house. An engineer familiar with the line explains that spent carbide is slaked lime and, if retained, it came in useful at the time of annual whitewashing of station premises.

6. Operational aspects

Accidents and incidents, C&WR

Operation was delightfully casual on the 9 miles of the C&WR, as seen during its last ten years of independence, from 1856 to 1865.

Driver James Shippen worked coal trains and was said to make a practice of having his engine on the main line when the passenger train was due, with collision only narrowly averted in one or two instances. He was reprimanded in September 1856, but a year later his pay was nevertheless increased to £1 10s 0d per week, albeit mainly to recognise the long hours he worked. William White, also an engine driver, and Hugh Dodd, his fireman, seem to have indulged in fisticuffs on the footplate (December 1857), the blame being placed on Dodd, who was reprimanded. Dodd had earlier been blamed for neglecting his engine on Sunday 8 March 1857, when the C&WR passenger train missed the 6.24pm from Workington to Carlisle, leaving mail bags and several passengers stranded. His downfall followed in March 1858 when, for the second time, he was found very drunk in charge of a passenger train, and was dismissed. His pay was 18 shillings weekly.

The other passenger fireman, William Christian, was severely reprimanded when the poor performance of his engine led to the Sunday evening connection for Carlisle and the south being missed on 21 June 1857. This time, a gentleman from London lodged a claim, but the C&WR Board maintained that 'he could have posted from Workington to Carlisle'. Christian again came to notice when, in June 1860, he fell from his engine, owing to being drunk on duty.

The pointsmen were few in number and easy-going by nature. J. Anderson was dismissed for failure to secure the points properly at Marron Siding on 30 August 1856; the engine of a passenger train from Workington was derailed, along with a wagon. In September 1858 Anderson's successor also was dismissed for allowing the horse-drawn coal wagons of Fletchers, the coal owners, on to the main line. In the same vicinity two or three coal wagons, probably of the chaldron type, were wrecked when, on 25 January 1859, they were blown out of Lowther Sidings into the path of the 9.00pm Workington-Cockermouth passenger train. Again, late on 18 December 1862, a Whitehaven Junction Railway locomotive collided with a C&WR wagon that had blown out of the Merchants' Quay branch on to the main line; the locomotive and the Derwent viaduct were damaged, and the wagon. Pointsman Wildman lost his job.

Finally, two successive station masters at Broughton Cross were dismissed (November and December 1862), the first for intemperate habits and the second for being very drunk on duty.

Confusion at the crossroads: Cockermouth Junction

One has long sympathised with railway signalmen in traditional cabins, when exposed to the problems of conflicting movements at times of heavy traffic. Probably, until recent years, the classic example was at Borough Market Junction, the dividing of the ways for Cannon Street and Charing Cross, London. But spare a thought also for the man in the much smaller signal box at Cockermouth Junction, a few years after the C&WR had become LNWR property and with the CKPR was still only eight years old. Traffic had expanded far beyond C&WR experience. The

An eastward view of Cockermouth passenger station from the road bridge. This view shows the scene just after closure in 1966, with the latter-day layout virtually intact. Note the water tower hidden amidst the trees on the right. *Harold D. Bowtell*

signal box was now described as a raised cabin, with steps, adequate signals and interlocking of points and signals, so it was presumably the new box of 1873.

On 14 April 1873 an M&CR passenger train from Cockermouth to the Brigham-Bullgill line ran past the box at 3.28pm. The driver helpfully signalled to the man in the box, by a display of fingers, that the LNWR passenger train from Penrith to Whitehaven, which should already have passed, was reported 18 minutes late from Penrith. The M&CR train was promptly followed down the 1 in 70 single-track bank from Cockermouth passenger station by a down light NER engine, then a down NER mineral train, comprising engine, 30 wagons of coke and a brake-van. These were disposed of, apart from the mineral brake-van, which was left for a time on the down running line.

Meanwhile, *two* up trains arrived on the double track route from the Workington direction, each with a LNWR engine and conveying, respectively, 29 and 18 mineral 'empties', bound from the West Cumberland

ironworks to County Durham. These trains were well behind time, as they had to be formed to provide a train for the two NER locomotives to take eastward, and by rights that would have been away at 3.05pm. Complicated shunting movements followed and they were overtaken by the appearance of the LNWR passenger train from Penrith at about 3.50pm. It was descending the bank faster than seemed prudent to eyewitnesses – the road being blocked by empty mineral wagons and the signals being at danger. The driver ran through the adverse signals at 15-18mph and collided with the wagons. Eight were damaged, of which three were derailed, while the engine's buffer beam was broken; 11 passengers were cut and bruised and 12 shaken. The passenger guard was hurt and so was the driver, who jumped from his engine. His train had been delayed at Penrith awaiting late-running main-line trains – *plus ça change*... The driver, Shippen, was stated to have worked on the line for 26 years and had been in LNWR service since 1866. He had thus joined the C&WR in its first year of operation, 1847; indeed, we have already met James Shippen in 1856. Lt-Col C. S. Hutchinson RE, inspecting officer for the Board of Trade, placed the blame on Driver Shippen (primarily), the signalman next (with some sympathy expressed), the lack of block working (note earlier references in the Signalling chapter), and on the inadequate braking of the passenger train, comprised of ten vehicles, of which two were brake-vans, but with only one guard conveyed.

Tragedy and comedy on the CKPR

The CKPR does not appear to have had any accidents to trains in which a passenger was killed, and few in which passengers suffered injury. Workers on the railway were, in relation to their numbers, far less fortunate. In the first year of operations (1865) platelayers James Thompson and John Pattinson were killed, in separate incidents; each widow received a gratuity of £5, and Mrs Pattinson was left with five children. In 1910 platelayer Thomas Gibson was killed. In 1906, Joseph Whitham, a porter signalman, lost his life at Troutbeck, run down by a light engine, his widow receiving 'the full compensation' of £156 under the Employers' Liability Act, by then effective. Porter Joseph Wilson was badly injured that year at Cockermouth station and, after investigating the circumstances, the Board of Trade pressed for a reduction of daily working hours to a maximum of 12. Locomotive firemen also died: at Troutbeck on 9 April 1873 NER footplateman Isaac Snowden fell from the front of his engine while running through on a mineral train; T. Dalton, LNWR, was killed at Cockermouth Junction on 14 December 1885; and at Bassenthwaite Lake station on 14 November 1898 LNWR fireman Gilbert Howard of Workington fell from the engine of a passing empty stock train after exchanging the tablet.

Conditions of the day – and of long after – at level crossings emerge from the death of Sarah Johnstone, killed on 17 January 1867 at Rakefoot, when helping her husband David, the official gatekeeper, by handling the gates. The rule was that the gates must be kept closed to the highway except when road vehicles required to cross and the keeper had to be on call 24 hours daily, but the company would employ only one person. Crossings at Bassenthwaite Lake (twice) and Embleton (on three occasions) figured in accidents.

A westward view at Troutbeck, looking down the bank towards Threlkeld (a double-track section) with the signal box behind the camera (see opposite). The bridge was demolished in 1984 and the road now crosses the formation at the former rail level. This picture was taken on 9 October 1966. *Harold D. Bowtell*

An interesting view at Troutbeck in BR days, which highlights both the bleak and rugged nature of the surrounding landscape, and also some unusual motive power. Fowler Class '4F' 0-6-0 No 44081 is seen just east of the platforms, shunting an up goods under the control of the 1874 Saxby & Farmer signal box. *Ainley collection/CRA*

Mechanical failures

Broken axles and other defects in wagons caused derailments, but on 22 May 1899 an LNWR passenger train engine broke its crank axle in Wythop cutting. On 22 August 1910 derailment while running followed failure of a spring of the leading pair of tender wheels on LNWR locomotive No 3069, an 0-6-0 ('Special DX'), working the 9.38am up passenger from Keswick.

Collisions and the human element

Collisions and 'near misses' occurred chiefly in the earlier days, from 1868 to 1896, and were usually due to the failure of pointsmen and others to set turnouts correctly.

On 23 October 1868 the passenger train due into Penrith at 5.00pm ran on to the turntable instead of into the station. An incident at Bassenthwaite Lake on 10 January 1889 led to the fixing – at this early period – of an electrical detector for the east-facing points, which were remote from the signal box, and similar protection was to be installed at Penruddock and Troutbeck.

Another weakness was revealed at Bassenthwaite Lake on 5 August 1901, when the driver of the 6.05pm up passenger service from Cockermouth ran into the station against signals. As a down train was approaching from the east and 'had the road' into the station, the west-facing points took the erring driver into the down platform – and the path of the oncoming locomotive. The trains were, fortunately, halted about 150 yards apart. Resulting refinements permitted entry of a down train without the west facing points being set for the down line.

There was also an incident at Keswick on 16 January 1896 when an early morning down NER mineral train, with S&DR '1001' Class 0-6-0 No 1184 in charge, ran past the unlit signals (doubtless at danger) into the up platform road, as an LNWR eastbound passenger train approached. Collision was only narrowly avoided, but No 1184 was derailed.

Disaster at Penruddock

By far the most serious collision occurred at Penruddock on Friday 2 September 1870. This was a gala day in Penrith, the racecourse being the scene of a review of four troops of the Yeomanry Cavalry. They were headed by Colonel Edward Hasell (1796-1872), of Dalemain, who had been Chairman of the Lancaster & Carlisle Railway at its opening in 1846. Four special trains had brought folk from West Cumberland and three trains returned at short intervals from Penrith

Making a smoky departure from Bassenthwaite Lake station in BR days, with a standard 20-ton brake-van attached, is Ivatt Class '2MT' 'Mickey Mouse' 2-6-0 No 46456, allocated to Workington shed (code 11B). Taken during the late 1950s, this interesting view from the signal box shows the neat station building on the down platform, and the immaculately manicured topiary on the up platform. The goods yard with its camping coaches (see opposite) is to the left. *Ivor Nicholas*

A familiar feature at 'Bass Lake' station for many post-war years was this pair of green-and-cream-liveried camping coaches, stabled in a disconnected siding in the goods yard. Each winter the adjacent siding was slewed to enable the vehicles to be taken to the works for refurbishing. Interesting detail includes the white-painted dustbin, the 'chocks' placed beneath the wheels to stop the carriages rolling, and the admirable neat and tidy condition of the site. A bottle of gas (for cookers, lights and, probably, heaters) can be seen in a special cage between the frames of the nearer vehicle, whose sole-bar carries a bold painted warning for railwaymen: 'No Brakes'. *Ivor Nicholas*

shortly after 7.00pm. The first of these comprised an engine and tender and about 15 carriages and was correctly held at Penruddock to cross the up Cockermouth-Penrith passenger, due there at 7.55pm. The second train was allowed to draw up close behind; it comprised an engine and tender and 39 carriages, plus brake-van, a horsebox containing three horses, and a second engine and tender attached at the rear.

The third train, with T. Smith driving and about 20 vehicles behind the engine, passed Penruddock's distant signal at danger (this being subsequently established, although Smith continued to deny it), and collided in the centre of the single-line viaduct with the double train (the second train, with the engine at the rear). The most serious damage was the near destruction of the last passenger carriage in the second train, but by great good fortune it had been standing outside the covered station at Penrith, in heavy rain, and

was empty. Three doctors on the train gave prompt assistance. More than £4,000 was paid in settling claims from injured passengers and, as is still the case today, arbitration was necessary to allocate liability between the CKPR and LNWR.

Runaways

The CKPR distinguished itself by a number of spectacular runaways. Dramatic episodes in BR days down the bank from Flusco and Blencow to Penrith were described in Volume 1, but there was also a westward runaway from Troutbeck in the 1940s. In CKPR days there had been six incidents, two of them westward from Troutbeck.

On Monday 13 February 1871 an up goods train reached Troutbeck, where the engine was detached; about 5 minutes later its train started to run back down the long and steep incline to Threlkeld and away through the gorge, speeding by Keswick and over the

lowlands, to come to rest beyond Braithwaite
– a distance of well over 10 miles – and
without harm.

The CKPR's second 'runaway spectacular'
occurred on Tuesday 18 April 1882, when
down NER mineral train No 6 left Keswick
westward that morning, with two tender
engines, 28 loaded coke wagons and two
brake-vans. As the train ran along the shore of
Bassenthwaite Lake, the 'ticket' of authority
for the section was duly carried. However,
both guards were (irregularly) riding in the
rear van and, when this became detached,
they were thus left to coast to a stand, while
the train proceeded, with a single unattended
brake-van at the rear, past Bassenthwaite Lake
station. Here the leading driver collected the
train staff for the next section. He soon noted
the absence of one brake-van but proceeded to
Embleton, whence the second engine took the
train forward to Cockermouth. He held the
staff for the section between Embleton and
Bassenthwaite Lake, so went back and joined
the head guard, who came up on foot, and the
station master. The latter knew that another
train was en route from Braithwaite, yet set off
with the driver, fireman and guard to find and

retrieve the missing van. After about a mile,
on a curve by the lake, the van was seen
approaching, propelled by the No 7 down
NER mineral train, which was duly carrying
the train staff for the section. The light engine
driver reversed, the other three leaped clear of
the footplate and the driver jumped (or was
knocked off) when the propelled van struck
his engine.

This locomotive had been reversed and
steam applied before impact and it now ran
away at speeds estimated at 40-60mph, passing
Bassenthwaite Lake, Rakefoot and Embleton
before running downhill to crash into the
M&CR's 1.25pm passenger train, which had
been ready to leave Cockermouth for Brigham
and Bullgill. It comprised an M&CR tender
engine and four vehicles. The last two
carriages were reduced to matchwood but,
happily, a telegraphed warning from Porter
Robinson at Bassenthwaite Lake to Clerk
Patterson at Cockermouth had been received
and acted upon with alacrity; this enabled the
railway staff to get all the passengers clear just
in time. The M&CR locomotive became
detached but a porter dashed after it, climbed
into the cab and brought it to a stand before it

An 'M&C' wagon is included in this pile-up of 'empties' just west of Bassenthwaite Lake station and level crossing
– the date is stated to be 1899. *Richard L. Pattinson/CRA*

accelerated down the very steep bank to the Junction, thereby averting yet greater tragedy.

Further runaways occurred during the years of the First World War. Trap points just east of Blencow on the bank down to Penrith saved the situation on 16 October 1916. A heavy down mineral train with two engines ran back when the drawbar of the leading (NER) wagon broke at Blencow. Had the trap points not been installed there would have been a fearful incident at the main-line junction. In the earlier days of single-track working east of Blencow there were no catch points and on 26 December 1889 the 6.00am double-headed down goods from Penrith stopped at Blencow to shunt. While the engines were detached most of the train ran back all the way downgrade to Penrith station, happily with few ill effects.

A far more spectacular runaway followed on Saturday 28 October 1916, at about 8.00pm. The No 30 up goods was heavily loaded and hauled by two engines ascending the bank to Troutbeck, when the rear coupling parted on an LNWR wagon – the second vehicle in the train. The brake-van at the rear could not hold the train, which ran away 'wrong line' down the bank. Guard Kirk, of Tebay, jumped for his life at Highgate Platform. The train, including 14 wagons loaded with steel shell cases from Workington, destined to be filled with explosives at the huge Ministry of Munitions factory at Gretna, derailed at the catch points in the cutting west of Highgate and an almighty pile-up resulted, partly on the lands of Highgate Farm. Mr Tyson, the farmer, ministered to the shocked guard with tea and his schoolgirl daughter Jessie clearly remembers the dramatic scene of the crash. It occurred close by the distinctive 'la'al pikey hut' – a superb Cumbrian description of the lineside cabin, which resembled a sentry box.

Just over a year later, on 13 December 1917, another runaway occurred. Fred Slee was conducting shunting movements at Troutbeck when, owing to a defective brake, Caledonian Railway gunpowder van No 20 (containing powder for use at Greenside lead mines) ran away down the bank, presumably 'right line' as it was not derailed by the Highgate catch points. The Highgate signalman warned Threlkeld, where the

In LMS days an up goods is climbing the long bank of almost 1 in 62 near Troutbeck, between Hill Cottages and Mosedale viaduct. This bank caused concern for the CKPR and LMS in terms of maintaining traffic flow towards Penrith at busy periods, and it was also the scene of several 'runaways'. *Richard L. Pattinson/CRA*

station master and his porter signalman placed sleepers across the line just beyond (west of) the station; the van approached, running at about 30mph, and pushed the sleepers ahead of it for a distance before stopping short of the overline bridge carrying the Penrith-Keswick road.

Hazard by fire

On the night of 1-2 August 1917 there was a fire in the screw-pile bridge at the Glenderamachin River, west of Threlkeld. Pending the eventual arrival of the Keswick Fire Brigade, good work was done by the station master and signalman, together with the porter and his wife, platelayer W. Lamb and Miss Julia Lamb, and Police Constable McMeithan.

Two gas tank wagons and an LNWR four-wheeled vehicle, all attached to the rear of the 2.05pm Workington-Penrith passenger train

of 22 November 1921, were derailed short of Blencow station and finally left the rails completely as they approached the platform. A fire followed, but Porter Bewley uncoupled the main portion of the train, which was thus drawn safely into the station. A joint enquiry by the CKPR and LNWR blamed the driver for allegedly running at excessive speed.

The snow fiend

Snow blocked this rugged railway route from time to time. This was chiefly at Gibson and Gillhead cuttings (west of Troutbeck), as well as at a point immediately west of Penruddock station and at three places between Penruddock viaduct and the western entry to Blencow station. Following the blockages of 28-31 January 1910, the CKPR wrote seeking advice from the Caledonian and Highland Railways, and members of the Board called on Sir Vincent Raven and his assistant at

A major problem with snow in St Andrews cutting, some half-mile west of Blencow station between MPs 26 and 27, with the locomotive facing Penrith and showing Low Fluskew Wood, in February 1932. The personalities (L-R) are William Storey, George Watson, the Keswick inspector (possibly Mr Dickinson), Bob Bainbridge and Anthony Horsley. In the tragedy of January 1940, at almost this point, three lives were lost in snow. *John Jameson, courtesy of Abbot Hall*

Darlington, viewing with them the NER's wooden snowploughs of 26 tons weight and a new 27-ton steel plough.

However, the CKPR's response was limited to the construction of additional stone walls and sleeper snow-fencing, which was extended in 1917. The lengthiest and most notable blockage involved the Keswick-Penrith section, which was impassable from Friday 26 January 1940. This led to a tragic mishap on Wednesday 31 January 1940 in St Andrews rock cutting, between Flusco and Blencow. A stranded engine with snowplough and another assisting engine had been dug out, after which the blocked cutting at St Andrews overline bridge was tackled by railway staff and some 80 soldiers. They were protected by detonators to eastward but, when empty wagons were propelled into the cutting, the detonators were either already buried in packed snow, or slid ahead of the wagons on the icy rails. There was no warning from these 'shots' and three men were killed outright when the wagons ran into the team of diggers: goods guards Bob Watson of Penrith and Joseph Hugill of Yanwath, and John Jardine White, a young soldier from Workington. Seven other people were slightly injured and many others barely escaped.

The exceptional snowfalls of 1947 caused blockage between Keswick and Penrith on 26 February and again on 13-14 March.

Railway links that might have been

We conclude this chapter with descriptions of some interesting proposed lines that never came to fruition. One of the earliest was the Cockermouth & Workington Extension Railway project of 1846, already touched on in the section detailing the building of the C&WR itself. Had it been built, it might have carried that line to Keswick, and even Windermere.

Around 1860 the M&CR had ideas of a route by way of Caldbeck to Penrith, but it was overtaken in 1861 by the CKPR's Act, followed closely by the building of the CKPR in the years 1862-64. Meanwhile, the CKPR in June 1864 had thought of connecting its line, in the Cockermouth-Embleton vicinity, with Ullock and the contemporary

developments from Cleator way; this thinking was not pursued and, as we know, the WC&ER made its own way north to Marron Junction in the course of another couple of years.

Attraction of the Midland Railway, 1867-1876

Encouraged by the MR Act of 16 July 1866 for the Settle & Carlisle main line, the CKPR proposed in February 1867 to survey a route from Penrith to (provisionally) Langwathby, which would transverse about 5 miles of easy country, but with a crossing of the River Eden. When the Midland failed to secure parliamentary approval to the abandonment of its Pennine main-line project, interest was revived in Penrith in the idea of a locally promoted link line. A committee was set up in April 1873, with the CKPR represented by directors Dover and Spedding, of Keswick. The committee's deliberations dragged on and eventually, in July 1876, the CKPR decided against giving support. By then, the Settle & Carlisle line was open to traffic. Right from the start the Midland intended to have, and indeed made, a physical link at Appleby with the NER Eden Valley line; this was, however, not exploited as a through route from the MR system (and Keswick) until the 20th century.

The Mid Cumberland Railway, 1881-1914

In 1881-82 an initiative came from London promoters under this title, designed to conjure up a picture of minerals being exploited in amazing variety. After a launch in the villages, Joseph Wilson, as Secretary of the promoters, addressed a letter to the CKPR. The miracle was to be achieved through the medium of a railway between Blencow (CKPR) and Mealsgate (M&CR), via Hesket Newmarket and Caldbeck. The CKPR compared notes with the M&CR; by October they decided that any line should be from Troutbeck station to Hesket Newmarket and points beyond, but they referred the proposal to a special meeting of shareholders. This was held at Keswick on 4 November 1882, when a decision against further consideration at that time was recorded.

Transport of minerals was of paramount importance in 19th-century Cumberland. This is an ex-works five-plank private owner wagon, of 10 tons capacity, belonging to the Cumberland Granite Company of Bassenthwaite Lake. The vehicle is marked with the inscription: 'When empty to Quarry Sidings, Embleton, CK&P Rly'. *Peter W. Robinson collection*

A fresh initiative came in May 1897 from L. R. Wilson of Manchester. This suggested a link between Troutbeck (CKPR) and Wigton station on the M&CR – with the title Mid Cumberland Light Railway – and for a couple of years exchanges continued. In November 1898 attention was concentrated on a shorter (branch) light railway, still under the same name, to extend from Troutbeck (or Penruddock) station to Hesket Newmarket and possibly onwards to Caldbeck. A cautious financial contribution by the CKPR was proposed by Directors James Cropper and Sir Henry Vane, the latter having an estate at Hutton-in-the-Forest near the route. However, the matter did not proceed beyond the early months of 1899. The Light Railways Act had been effective since 1 January 1897, and had probably inspired the scheme, but no Order for the line was secured under the Act.

Note also the plans of 1904, and traffics through later years, for the Carrock Mines (J. Wright Wilson, of Penrith, promoter),

mentioned in Volume 1 in reference to Troutbeck station. In January-April 1900 a proposed quarry branch from Troutbeck to near Carrick Fell (meaning Carrock Fell?) was also raised with the railway company by a widely based deputation, but it did not gain CKPR support. Surprisingly, in November 1914, a letter from Mr A. E. Beck to the company mentioned a proposed line from 'Carrick End', but this was not elaborated or developed.

The Braithwaite & Buttermere Railway, 1880-1883

The Buttermere Green Slate Company have for long quarried attractive and high quality Lake District slate near Honister Pass, between Buttermere and Borrowdale. In 1880 the company was looking for expansion, but a governing factor was the cost of transporting their output by horse-drawn two-wheeled carts to Keswick station. If cheaper transport could be arranged, the company believed it could find a market for lower-quality slate and boost its current output of 50-100 tons weekly to around 400 tons. This would be achieved, they reasoned, by a railway between the Honister quarries and Braithwaite station. The proposition was put to the CKPR in June 1880. The slate folk hinted at the 'competitive' options of an extension of the Rowrah & Kelton Fell Railway or a line up Ennerdale, each of these reaching Honister from the west, but they were hardly realistic alternatives and the CKPR was not inspired to offer encouragement.

Undeterred, the Slate Company proceeded to 'sound' the LNWR and, in November-December 1881, came back with a proposal. CKPR Chairman Spedding, of Keswick, and his colleague Captain Henry Gandy, of Penrith, met at Carnforth on 7 November 1881 with five Directors of the Slate Company – Messrs Poole (solicitor), Massicks, Cook, Swan and Storey. Edward Waugh MP was a member of the Slate Board and, after years as solicitor to the railway, was by this time listed in their Board too. He was later revealed to be in favour of the scheme, but very correctly did not attend the meeting. A railway of about 2-foot gauge and some 8 miles in length was proposed, to pass along the slopes of Cat Bells, above the western shore of Derwentwater. The railway's response was still very cautious. The quarry company promoted a Bill but it was withdrawn in April 1883, following four months of attacks, progressively fiercer and better organised, as the Reverend H. D. Rawnsley, at that time still Vicar of Wray, on Windermere, led the campaign on behalf of the 'environmentalists' of the day. No more was heard of the intriguing narrow-gauge steam line from Braithwaite to Honister; Buttermere was always a misnomer.

A Solway Junction proposal

Contemporary with the Honister scheme was a plan for a railway from the north. The Solway Junction Railway, with its long, lightly used and flimsy viaduct over the Solway estuary undergoing three years of repairs after damage by ice, sought in November 1882-January 1883 to interest the CKPR in a joint scheme. This was for the promotion of a Bill to permit construction of a line to reach Bassenthwaite Lake station. Potential traffic from Scotland to the Lake District was mentioned encouragingly, but the CKPR did not approve of the proposed layout at Bassenthwaite Lake and liked still less the suggestion in the draft Bill (of January 1883) for running powers over its line. They probably had doubts too as to whether the Solway Junction Company seriously intended to press on as far south as Bassenthwaite Lake. The scheme came to naught.

7. The locomotive story

Locomotives of the C&WR

During its independent working career, from 1847 to 1866, the C&WR owned six locomotives, two at its opening in April 1847, three by the autumn of that year (reduced to two by a sale in 1853), again increased to three in 1854, then four by mid-1856 and a maximum of five from 1864. These five were taken into the LNWR 'capital list' in December 1866 and allotted LNWR numbers, although the first LNWR numbers (12/1866) were never carried, representing a paper transaction only. Incidentally, numbers between 1 and 5 have been quoted for the engines in C&WR stock, but that company always referred to them by names; the numbers may have been introduced by LNWR locomotive historian S. S. Scott.

The following accounts derive from my own reading and interpretation of the C&WR's surviving minutes and the broadly parallel (and earlier) findings of Mr E. Craven from that source, along with information from LNWR sources.

Derwent (1846)

This was an 0-4-2 tender locomotive with 4ft 9in diameter coupled wheels and cylinders (probably inside) of 14in x 21in built by Tulk & Ley, of Lowca. It was ordered in January 1846 and received by the C&WR in October 1846, being the makers' eighth locomotive. Derwent was found too heavy and disposal was in mind by 1850; it was eventually sold in 1853, possibly to the Whitehaven & Furness Junction Railway (derived from a suggestion in the records of LNWR locomotive historian S. S. Scott).

Cocker

Cocker was also an 0-4-2 tender locomotive with 4ft 9in diameter coupled wheels and inside cylinders of 13in x 18in. The locomotive was built by Alfred Kitching of Darlington, quoted as their No 15, ordered on 2 March 1846 and delivered either in December 1846 or January 1847; it was promptly loaned to J. & W. Ritson, the C&WR's contractors, to supplement their own locomotive during the completion and ballasting of the line.

On 14 May 1847 the C&WR was complaining to the makers that this locomotive could not perform its work satisfactorily, alleging a defect in the pumps – presumably referring to a boiler feed pump. A valve gear with expansion links, such as Stephenson's gear, was probably fitted in 1852. Early in 1857 the locomotive was rebuilt as an 0-4-0 with a lengthened coupled wheelbase, lengthened firebox and new cylinders (13in x 22in). Following conversion, on 31 March 1857 it figured in a dramatic mishap. In the run-up to a parliamentary election at Cockermouth, the C&WR ran special trains, and Cocker was hauling a 'special' of 11 carriages and a van, carrying about 300 passengers. The train was returning from Cockermouth to Whitehaven and was seemingly just clear of the viaducts in the Salmon Hall vicinity (below Seaton) when the engine 'split the road' and rolled over the right-hand bank, coming to rest facing east. The fireman was injured and the Company Secretary, John Mayson, was severely injured, but passengers in the carriages appear to have escaped. Captain H. W. Tyler RE, of the Board of Trade inspectorate, was scathing in his comments on

Cocker is here depicted around 1890-93. The location is between Cowburn Tunnel East and Edale, on the Dore &
Chinley Railway (MR), while under construction. This (westerly) portion of the line was being built by contractor
J. P. Edwards, but Thomas Oliver (observe the 'TO' on the wagons) was engaged between Hathersage and Dore,
the eastern end of the new line. MR, *courtesy of J. B. Radford*

the design of the engine, the condition of the
viaduct and of the permanent way.

More misfortune followed; *Cocker* broke its
crank axle on 23 November 1858, with delay
to traffic (the report suggests that it was
hauling a passenger train at the time). The
axle was presumably renewed.

The locomotive was again rebuilt in March
1866 (this time by the LNWR at Crewe),
when it acquired new (lengthened) inside
frames, the cylinders being enlarged to 13in x
22in and the boiler replaced. Its LNWR
numbering was 1550 in December 1866, 1577
in April 1867, 1259 in July 1867, and 1821 in
November 1871. *Cocker* was sold by the
LNWR (possibly through the agency of
Fletcher Jennings) in March 1874 to well-
known railway contractor Joseph Firbank,
initially (it would seem) at Camden. The
engine was resold to J. P. Edwards and rebuilt
for him at Crewe in January 1886, when the
tender was removed and a saddle tank
substituted. The wheel arrangement was still
0-4-2, with inside cylinders.

It worked on construction of the Brighton
& The Dyke Railway, 1886-87, being in the

Brighton Works of the LB&SCR in March
and April 1887 for repairs and the fitting of a
wooden cab and windows to the contractor's
order. The cylinders are recorded as 15in x
24in by this time – it is not known whether or
not this is accurate. The locomotive was with
Edwards during building of the Nottingham
Suburban Railway (GNR), 1886-89; and the
Dore & Chinley Railway (MR), probably
during the years 1890-93. It was photographed
there hauling an inspection train towards the
end of that time, when outside frames and the
wooden cab were noted. After this *Cocker*
disappears from the records, its ultimate fate
unknown.

Marron

This 0-4-2 tender engine with 4ft 9in
diameter coupled wheels and 13in x 18in
inside cylinders was built by Alfred Kitching
of Darlington, believed to be works No 16 and
delivered in 1847, probably during August. In
March 1847, while still on order, the C&WR
Board suggested to John Dixon that 14-inch
diameter cylinders might produce a more
powerful engine, but Mr Dixon considered

this an affront to his technical judgement and threatened to resign forthwith; the Board hastily withdrew the proposal. *Marron* was regarded as a mineral locomotive.

In 1852 the coupled wheels were re-tyred and link motion was probably fitted. The engine became very run-down in 1856; a broken crank axle was replaced towards the end of 1856 and major repairs were done in 1857-58, together with a 'rebuilding' in 1861. The cylinders were bored to a larger diameter in March 1867, at Crewe, although the 0-4-2 wheel arrangement was retained and, presumably, the tender.

The locomotive's LNWR numbering was 1549 in December 1866, 1576 in April 1867, 1147 in July 1867, and 1822 in November 1871. Between July 1867 and at least July 1871 No 1147 (quoted as an 0-4-2 tank) worked on the High Peak line. As No 1822 it was sold by the LNWR in February 1874 to William Horsley Jnr, of Newcastle-upon-Tyne, who had his business at Whitehill Point. He may well have bought the locomotive on behalf of the owners of the Brunton & Shields wagonway, which in 1886 became the Seaton Burn Coal Company's wagonway for bringing coals from its collieries in Northumberland, down to the north bank of the Tyne for shipment.

Derwent (1854)

This was the second locomotive of this name on the C&WR, and was a 4ft 9in 2-4-0T, with outside cylinders (12in x 18in), built by Neilson, of Glasgow (Works No 75 of 1854). It was delivered new to the C&WR and known as 'the small tank engine', probably used for passenger duties. Its LNWR numbering was 1548 in December 1866, 1575 in April 1867, and 1192 in July 1867. *Derwent* was broken up by the LNWR on 18 June 1868, this being some 18 months after the take-over, with 'boiler very bad, frame patched, etc'.

Solway

This 5ft 0in 0-4-0ST, with outside cylinders (14in x 20in), was built by Neilson as Works No 324 of 1856 and delivered new to the C&WR. It was intended as a mineral engine but at once proceeded to do the line and its weak bridges little good, while fracturing its own frames. Neilson declined to accept responsibility for its shortcomings, attributing these to the specification of John Dodds, who tendered his resignation as Secretary, Manager and Engineer of the C&WR in May 1856, effective 12 August. The subsequent report states: 'She was a tank engine of great overhanging weight, the framing was too light and of poor workmanship, and soon fractured.' One may surmise that Dodds and Neilson 'boosted' the size of wheels and cylinders, and saddle tank, to convert Neilson's contemporary design of 'pug engine' from an industrial yard shunter into a mineral engine for main-line trip working.

Rebuilding was by R. & W. Hawthorn, of Newcastle-upon-Tyne, with a shorter coupled wheelbase and a pair of 3ft 3in carrying wheels, together with a tender supplied by Sharp Stewart, of Manchester, around the end of 1856. The locomotive later appeared in Crewe records as a 2-4-0 tender engine. Its LNWR numbering was 1547 in December 1866, 1574 in April 1867, and 1183 in July 1867. *Solway* was broken up by the LNWR on 18 June 1868 (the boiler having been scrapped in November 1867), thus enjoying an even shorter survival after take-over than the second *Derwent*. This was the most obscure locomotive owned by the C&WR.

Eller

Eller was a 4ft 9in 0-6-0 tender engine with inside cylinders (15in x 24in), built by Hudswell Clarke, of Leeds (Works No 28 of 1864, its tender being HC No 29). It was dispatched on 27 August 1864 from the works to the C&WR carrying *Eller* nameplates on the boiler cladding. This was the only six-coupled loco of the C&WR and of more sturdy dimensions and weight than its predecessors; Mr Tosh, as engineer, would be influenced by increasing mineral loads and the rebuilding of the river bridges. The cylinders were of 15⅜in diameter by 1871.

The loco's LNWR numbering was 1546 in December 1866, 1573 in April 1867, 1185 in December 1867, and 1823 in November 1871.

The last of the six locomotives built for the Cockermouth & Workington Railway was *Eller*, of 1864, built by Hudswell Clarke of Leeds and seen at that company's works as a new engine. *R. N. Redman collection*

Eller was scrapped by the LNWR on 7 May 1881, having survived nearly 15 years in LNWR stock.

During October-December 1858 coal-firing was substituted for coke in all four locomotives of the time and Mr Tosh reported a saving of £248 17s 9d in fuel costs during the following half-year, representing a 60% reduction on the previously recorded expenditure. Coal was always cheaper than coke, but the railways had previously opted for coke because of pressure to minimise the smoke nuisance.

Passenger carriages

The C&WR had four passenger carriages built by Atkinson & Phillipson for its opening in 1847. These comprised two 1st Class vehicles, one 2nd Class coach and a Composite. In 1856 and after there were eight carriages: two 1st, two 2nd and four 3rd Class vehicles. Two more carriages were added to the stock list in 1864-65. The June 1856 inventory also showed 14 merchandise trucks (increased to 20 a year later), 302 coal and lime chaldron wagons, six stone wagons, a travelling crane with 'fly bogies', two horses, three carts and a road wagon.

Arrival of LNWR engines and men

From the start of regular passenger and goods traffic over the new CKPR, in January 1865, the LNWR provided engines and footplate crews, which involved operation from Penrith to Cockermouth and back. With the LNWR take-over of the West Cumberland lines from mid-1866 it soon became necessary for LNWR locomotives to work between Penrith, Cockermouth, Workington and Whitehaven, effectively from about the beginning of 1867.

LNWR locomotives would be based at Penrith, presumably stabled in the open until the engine shed was built. From 1867 they would have had the use of the former Whitehaven Junction Railway's restricted facilities at Whitehaven (Bransty) for stabling and servicing engines. There was said in 1855 to be a turntable, south of the station, at Workington, but it is not apparent on the map of 1864. The first known shed available to LNWR engines in Workington was a six-road structure built in 1876. It acquired LNWR number 32 in September 1877 and was doubled in size, to 12 roads, under authority of 1890, continuing in use for steam power until closure wef 1 January 1968. Some stabling at Cockermouth is implied by the passenger train service of the 1860s; CKPR services in

1865 would require as a minimum one Penrith-based engine making two return trips daily to Cockermouth and one engine based at Cockermouth to make a return trip to Penrith. Goods would presumably be worked from Penrith. The integrated CKPR-LNWR passenger service of 1867 embraced six or seven trains each way on the C&WR section and three each way on the CKPR, including two up and three down through trains. In general, the services operated to and from Whitehaven. Even so, Cockermouth would have to provide power for the early 6.35am to Penrith and the 7.50am to West Cumberland; in later years, a Workington engine ran out 'light' to take this morning 'commuter' train.

Once Workington shed was open (from 1876-77) it undertook the lion's share of locomotive duties on the Workington-Penrith route. By the 20th century there was a consistent allocation of around 20 locomotives at Workington for Keswick line work (and others reserved for coastal line and local work). Penrith shed provided between five and seven engines for the Keswick line. Workington's contribution declined in 1948 to about 15, and during the years 1950-54 it fell further to eight, an allocation curtailed even more as DMU trains took over most passenger work, commencing in January 1955

under a scheme fully effective by 1956. Penrith shed closed entirely wef 18 June 1962, by which time the diesel sets were mostly running through between Workington and Carlisle, via Penrith.

The identity of the LNWR locomotives working the Cockermouth and Keswick route between the mid-1860s and the 1880s is lost in the mists of time. However, it seems reasonable to suppose that the early engines would be of the 'Crewe Goods' 5-foot 2-4-0 tender type (first built at Crewe in 1846), with outside cylinders (15in x 20in) within their distinctive wrapper; also the 'Crewe Goods Side Tank', a somewhat rudimentary 2-4-0 side tank conversion of 1856 onwards. Based on the 2-4-0 'Crewe Goods' design were 20 5-foot engines with 17in x 20in cylinders, by Rothwell, and seven with 17in x 24in cylinders, by Fairbairn, all built for the Lancaster & Carlisle Railway in 1856-59. Some of these engines could well have worked on the Keswick road in the period from 1865 to about 1880.

Established locomotive types on the route

Obvious candidates for the route, likewise suitable for passenger or goods traffic in the days before the continuous train brake, were

This is the LNWR steam shed at Workington, in LMS times, on 3 August 1946, when little had changed structurally. The 'northlight' roof covers all 12 roads. The varied locomotives outside are (L-R) an LMS standard '4F' 0-6-0, a Midland Railway 0-6-0 (tender seen), an LNWR '18-inch Goods' 0-6-0, a Lancashire & Yorkshire Railway 0-6-0 and an LMS Fowler 2-6-2T. *Harold D. Bowtell*

the substantial 0-6-0 tender engines of the 'DX' type, with 5-foot wheels and 17in x 24in cylinders. They were built in huge numbers for the LNWR between 1858 and 1872 and were favoured by the Northern and North Eastern Divisions. A sloped-back smokebox with a horizontally hinged door, ornamental chimney and the absence of a cab were characteristic features of the class, although a hint of sophistication was present in the later examples built. Cabs were fitted during the 1870s and this was doubtless appreciated in Cumberland.

As rebuilt from 1881, the 'DX' became the 'Special DX'; in this form Webb boilers were fitted, with 150psi boiler pressure, and there were also cabs. The fitting of the automatic vacuum brake was the most vital improvement, from about 1887 onwards; the last non-vacuum example was eliminated from LNWR stock in 1902. The 'Special DX' was the class of locomotive remembered far back on the Keswick route and illustrated in

the years before 1910 working both passenger and goods over the line. An observer in August 1920 recorded five of these locomotives between Penrith and Keswick, all of which were later withdrawn by the LMS between 1921 and 1926. Two are known to have been allocated to Workington in 1912 and five in 1917, while indications are that about five continued to share the line's work (from Penrith and Workington sheds) until early LMS days, about 1925.

The 'DX' and 'Special DX' were supported by the 4ft 6in 2-4-2 side tanks (cylinders 17in x 20in), built by Crewe in this form from 1879, and we have photographic evidence of one at work on CKPR passenger duties before 1893 , so some of these may well have arrived new in the 1880s to work the passenger trains. Cecil J. Allen was told when visiting in 1921 that the line 'used to employ 2-4-2 tanks'.

Another class of tank engine had a long career on the line. This was the eminently suitable 4ft 3in 'Side Tank Coal' of 0-6-2

The LNWR 'Special DX' 0-6-0s provided the prime passenger and goods motive power for the CKPR and C&WR lines through most of their history prior to LMS days (1923), and indeed ran for a little longer. This example, No 3331, was built as LNWR No 358 *Falstaff*, third of a huge class in 1858. It ran as No 3331 from 1900 and was finally withdrawn by the LMS in January 1928. The loco is seen at Penrith engine shed, pleasantly posed. *James L. Slater collection*

It is good to see a tank engine on CKPR passenger duties in the last century: this is an LNWR 4ft 6in 2-4-2T on a train of early LNWR stock. As seen here, these engines were built with a horizontally hinged smokebox door (an inconvenient arrangement for the enginemen and shed staff) c1879-83, and the train is entering Troutbeck through the single-track arch of Matterdale Road bridge, before the doubling of 1893-94. This may well be a scene before electric tablet working; one cannot see the type of 'staff' or 'tablet' that is about to be handed out. *Courtesy of Abbot Hall*

design with inside cylinders (17in x 24in) built by the LNWR in goodly numbers from 1881 onwards and employed in West Cumberland and on the Keswick road certainly by the 1890s, and probably also during the previous decade. They were included for many years in Penrith's modest allocation but their stronghold was at Workington; 14 examples were there in the 1912 list, 16 in 1917, probably much the same in 1919-20, still eight in 1933 and four in 1934. They were useful for 'trip' duties within reach of Workington, as well as for goods as far afield as Cockermouth and Keswick. The 5ft 6in 2-4-2 tanks (with 17in x 24in cylinders) do not appear to have come to Workington in their earlier years – they were built between 1890 and 1897. They came, it is believed, in the years 1919-20, and worked the occasional through passenger journey to Penrith. Workington had three examples in the 1930s and two in 1945-46. The engines ended their days on light van trains, but they were

previously found on the Bullgill-Brigham-Cockermouth (and sometimes Keswick) passenger services, which connected with the M&CR Carlisle trains at Bullgill and which conveyed a carriage for Carlisle. The M&CR's sole 0-4-4 well tank loco, No 26, is understood to have worked to Cockermouth from Bullgill; it was built in 1897 and withdrawn by the LMS in 1925.

This brings us to the engines that will be associated with the Keswick road as long as it is remembered – the 'Cauliflowers', strictly '18 inch Goods' of 0-6-0 tender type, with 5-foot diameter coupled wheels and 18in x 24in inside cylinders. They were notable for pioneering the use of David Joy's inside valve gear when F. W. Webb (at Crewe) introduced the design in 1880; the gear was retained throughout their long lives. For Keswick line duties they were based at Penrith but were allocated in far greater numbers at Workington, taking over progressively from the 'Special DX', with which design they

Above The LNWR '18-inch Goods' 0-6-0, or more familiarly 'Cauliflower', was the type that, after the 'Special DX', became most associated with the Keswick line. Many have been illustrated and here is an excellent view of No 8526 at Keswick, with an up passenger train. *LGRP*

Below Two successive generations of Keswick road staple motive power are illustrated here. 'Cauliflower' No 28417 is keeping company with a very new arrival, Ivatt '2MT' 2-6-0 No 46455, at Penrith engine shed on 13 August 1950. Penrith Beacon is on the skyline, seen to the left of the shed roof. *Neville Fields*

shared the 5-foot wheels. They were established by the time of the First World War, with six examples allocated at Workington in 1912 and seven in 1917, rising to 19 at the shed through most of the years 1930-47, falling back into 14 in 1948, four in 1950 and none in 1954. Concurrently, Penrith commonly had six or seven, the last two examples here being replaced late in 1954. Until then one of these engines was likely to appear on the Penrith-Keswick goods turn. For years Workington contrived to reserve a 'Cauliflower', fresh from Crewe Works in the spring, to work 'The Lakes Express' during the following summer.

It was the limitations of many bridges – discussed elsewhere in this work – that restricted the axle loading permitted on the line and thus the locomotive types employed. This was why the only express passenger locomotives employed in LNWR days were the 2-4-0 tender engines so well-known as 'Jumbos' and affectionately remembered by older enginemen for their lively and economical performance.

It is probable that the first examples were based at Workington from about the time when 'Jumbos' were demoted from express duties to main-line assisting locomotives and secondary-line services, around 1900 or perhaps a little later. There were none at Workington in 1896 but Nos 793 *Martin* and 1166 *Wyre* were based at the shed on 9 November 1912, as were Nos 124 *Marquis Douro* and 739 *Ostrich* in October 1917. *Ostrich* was observed to be active on the route in August 1920. *Sister Dora* went ex-works from Crewe to Workington, still as LNWR No 2158, in December 1924 and probably stayed until withdrawal from service in September 1927. LNWR No 424 *Sirius* (allotted LMS number 5107, but broken up in July 1927) had a spell at Workington shed and ran on the Keswick road.

The pattern of allocating a couple of the 6-foot-coupled-wheel variant to Workington was probably constant until LMS Nos 5102 *Cuckoo* and 5104 *Woodlark* were withdrawn from that shed in 1931. It was a delight when, for my first journey from Penrith to Keswick in June 1930, *Woodlark* figured at the head of five varied bogie carriages and made a faultless run into the evening sun. The 6ft 6in-wheeled variant appeared from Penrith shed and on through workings at busy times from Carlisle; for example, No 1675 *Vimiera* is illustrated in June 1919, captured by Ken Nunn, and W. E. Boyd found No 2193 *Salopian* regularly at work in August 1920. Penrith, formerly a sub-depot of Workington, was controlled by Carlisle (Upperby) from 1923, using shed number 29 (like Upperby) for some years, indeed nominally 29P. Around 1930 the line was favoured by 'Jumbos', which were perhaps

An LNWR-design 2-4-0, running in post-Grouping condition as LMS No 25001 *Snowdon*, is seen at Troutbeck on 10 September 1934. This locomotive is remembered with affection as it was the last 'Jumbo' in passenger service anywhere on the LMS system; it was based at Penrith shed and worked the Keswick road until withdrawal in October 1934. *A. St G. Walsh collection*

numerically in the ascendant, but not for long. In 1932 Nos 5001 *Snowdon* and 5050 *Merrie Carlisle* were based at Penrith for a time, No 5050 being withdrawn in 1933 (from Carlisle), while *Snowdon* remained at Penrith and was in regular use on Keswick line passenger trains until close on withdrawal in October 1934. By that time the engine was numbered 25001 and was often prominent as seen from passing expresses.

Midland and LMS/BR locomotives

The LMS brought in a few of the former MR 2-4-0 express locomotives; No 185 came to Penrith shed in 1933 and No 87 joined it in 1934. In the autumn of 1935 Nos 185 and 20087 (which derived from 87) were present. They were permitted over the bridges throughout from Penrith to Keswick and Workington but were employed mainly on stopping passenger trains from Penrith to Carlisle, or double-heading with a 'Cauliflower' between Carlisle and Keswick.

From 1946 the LMS and BR built light 2-6-0 locomotives (classed '2F', later '2MT') with 5-foot diameter coupled wheels and outside cylinders (16in x 24in), Walschaerts valve gear, rocking grate and hopper ashpan and a superheated boiler, the maximum axle load being about 13½ tons. They arrived on the Keswick road from late 1950 and in due course four examples were at Penrith, while eight examples at Workington virtually monopolised the route. After the introduction of DMUs in 1955-56 their numbers were reduced and thereafter they chiefly worked 'The Lakes Express' and goods duties.

This class was popularly given the nickname 'Mickey Mouse', doubtless because of their perky appearance and performance. At Upperby, a shed that worked 'Pacifics', they were known as 'Penrith Lizzies'. Their maximum load was usually six bogies of 57-foot stock; my train of five more variable-length stock with *Woodlark* will be recalled for comparison.

Some daily and occasional workings

While the daily passenger duties for engines and men were usually end-to-end between

One of the MR 2-4-0 locos that infiltrated Carlisle-Penrith-Keswick workings. This is believed to be No 20185, which came to the district in 1933 as No 185. The train is coming off the Cockermouth line at Derwent Junction, Workington – an MR 2-4-0 would not be common at the western end of the route. The overline bridge, No 45A of about 1904, is at the rear of the train and on the left is a long terrace of ironworks cottages. *Richard L. Pattinson/CRA*

Penrith and Workington and vice versa, the goods train duties were normally booked as follows: Workington to Cockermouth and return, and Workington to Keswick and return, both worked by Workington men; Penrith to Cockermouth and return, and Penrith to Keswick and return, both worked by Penrith men.

In 1906 the locomotive on 'duty 24' to Cockermouth was employed from 12 noon until 1.45pm for shunting the coal depots and warehouse sidings. If the midday 'fast goods' from Workington to Penrith required assistance, the duty 24 engine would interrupt its shunting to 'bank' the train from Cockermouth Junction to Embleton, then returning light engine to the Junction and yard. In LMS days 'the Keswick goods' duty for Workington men was quite a tough assignment owing to the number of shunting calls, typically at William Pit Sidings, Camerton Brickworks, Brigham, Cockermouth Yard, Cockermouth Gas Works Siding, Cockermouth Cattle Sidings and Oil Tank Siding, Embleton (as required), Close Quarry Siding, Bassenthwaite Lake, Braithwaite and Keswick, where it met the Penrith-Keswick goods for exchange of traffic. If the return goods to Penrith produced an overload, the Workington locomotive banked it all the way to Penruddock, then returned to Keswick, turned, and collected its homeward traffic.

From Penrith a change in locomotive duties

is found between 1906 and 1921, owing to the coming of the eight-hour working day. The engine of the 'traditional' mid-morning goods from Penrith to Keswick (then 11.10am) was booked in 1906 to leave Keswick again at 5.55pm, light engine for Threlkeld, and to bring the 6.20pm Threlkeld-Penrith goods home, due at 7.45pm. In 1921 a return into Penrith at 5.55pm (booked) was specified. In the latter days of the CKPR, c1918-22, the mid-afternoon goods from Penrith to Keswick was commonly worked by Penrith men with an 0-6-2 'Coal' tank, returning in the early evening from Keswick. In late LMS days the very early morning goods from Penrith, successor to the 'mixed train' of old, was worked through to Cockermouth by Penrith men, who came back with the morning goods of the time from Cockermouth Yard to Penrith. They were supposed to conclude with out-and-back 'trip' workings to Clifton Moor then Southwaite to shunt the respective station yards, but this proved to make an excessively long day. It may be noted that Penrith men normally came off down goods trains at Cockermouth passenger station, in order to turn their engine, before continuing with the train to the Junction and Cockermouth (lower) Yard.

An interesting sidelight on the working of passenger trains is provided in the LNWR 'Appendix', as shown in the accompanying table. The omission from the table of 6-foot and 6ft 6in 'Jumbo' 2-4-0 locomotives may

LNWR 'Appendix', April 1916: 'Passenger trains; CK&P Railway'

	Small tank engines	Goods engines, 18-inch tanks, side-tank coal	Max permitted four- or six-wheeled passenger vehicles
Workington-Cockermouth	160 tons	200 tons	16
Cockermouth-Keswick	160 tons	200 tons	11*
Keswick-Troutbeck	135 tons	170 tons	9*
Troutbeck-Penrith	160 tons	200 tons	16*
Penrith-Troutbeck	135 tons	170 tons	9*
Troutbeck-Workington	160 tons	200 tons	16 *

*Without bank engine

indicate that they were not usually working over the line in that year, although this does seem surprising. An excursion train from Edinburgh Waverley by the LNER Waverley Route was reported on 18 May 1936, arriving at Carlisle behind NBR 'Atlantic' No 9906 *Teribus*. The train ran forward to Keswick hauled by Midland Class '2' (Belpaire) 0-6-0 No 3655 (acquired by Upperby from the recently closed Durran Hill shed) as pilot to 'Cauliflower' No 8415. One evening in August 1938 (or possibly 1939) a return excursion came off the Keswick line at Penrith with a 'Cauliflower' and 2-4-0 No 185; the train ran to Carlisle behind No 185 unaided, 'out of section' being received in about 7 minutes.

In about 1928 John Roberts fired on a 'Cauliflower' that took over its special passenger train at Springs Branch, south of Wigan, bound for the Keswick Convention. The load was about six bogies and the route was via the LNER link line between Eamont Junction and Redhills Junction. A conductor joined the train at Eamont box and the water

picked up from the troughs at Dillicar (before Tebay) lasted to Keswick. An amusing 'Cauliflower' working from the western end of the line, in the 1930s, concerned an excursion run via the Furness coastal route to the 'Manchester November Handicap'. On returning to Workington, late at night, a Workington 'Cauliflower' was booked to take the front vehicles forward to Keswick, returning as empty stock in the early hours of the morning. On returning, the train crashed through the gates at Rakefoot crossing, the gatekeeper being asleep – and the driver too?

'The big engines'

It was reported that in 1936 a large tank engine of a highly competent class was run on the Keswick line – No 2313, once *The Prince*, a 2-6-4T. The progressive bridge strengthening between Penrith and Keswick would be nearing completion at this time and this was probably some form of trial. The bridge-strengthening programme was never extended west of Keswick, but was finished thus far by 1938, when '4F' 0-6-0 engines were

'The big engines' are here represented by No 45559 **British Columbia**, a '5X' 'Jubilee' three-cylinder 4-6-0, described by the photographer as toiling up the 1 in 70 gradient past Blencow station; this is not surprising with ten vehicles of mostly BR Mk 1 stock. The train is the Newcastle-Keswick, on 23 June 1957. *Robert Leslie*

6.30pm Keswick-Newcastle
'Royal Scot' Class '7P' 4-6-0 No 46136 *The Border Regiment*
10 coaches (327/345 tons)
Sunday 18 August 1957

Miles	Timing point	Schedule	Actual	Speed	
0.0	KESWICK	0	0.00		1 min late
1.0	Briery Mill Halt		3.54	24	
2.0	Milepost 15		6.04	28	
3.0	Milepost 16		7.53	40	
3.5	Threlkeld	9	8.38	30	
4.0	Milepost 17		9.49	28	
4.5	Milepost 17½		10.53	27	
5.0	Milepost 18		11.55	31	
5.5	Milepost 18½		13.05	26	
6.0	Milepost 19		14.11	28	
6.5	Milepost 19½		15.15	29	
7.0	Milepost 20		16.18	27	
7.5	Milepost 20½		17.24	26	
8.0	Milepost 21		18.29	27	
8.2	Troutbeck		19.00	31	
8.5	Milepost 21½		19.32	28	
9.5	Milepost 22½		20.59	54	
10.5	Penruddock	26	22.23	25/34	
11.0	Milepost 24		23.18	31/50	
12.0	Milepost 25		24.41	47	
13.0	Flusco Siding		25.47	62	
14.4	Blencow	33	27.51	28	
15.2	Catch points		28.54	48	
16.6	Redhills Junction		30.29	64	
17.8	Penrith No 1		32.27	20	
18.2	PENRITH	39	33.24		

Maximum equivalent drawbar horsepower: 1635

Log courtesy of H. G. Ellison

authorised to run to Keswick. The first example arrived on the London (Euston)-Keswick Convention special working of 15 July 1938. Incidentally, a '4F' would be a doubtful advance on a 'Cauliflower' in good order. A driver who endeavoured to work a heavy wartime train for Roedean schoolgirls with a '4F' suffered tribulations, shortages of steam and stops to 'blow up' on the grades.

The new 60-foot turntable at Keswick made possible the first working of a 'Black 5' 4-6-0 in the summer of 1939. During and after the 1939-45 war a '5MT' very occasionally worked a Penrith-Keswick goods. More regular, after the war, was the summer Saturday morning working of the Keswick-Manchester train by a 2-6-4T from Oxenholme shed. It was detached at Penrith and worked the Euston-bound 'Lakes Express', which had come from Workington behind one or two 'Cauliflowers', south to Oxenholme.

As the NER Redhills-Eamont link had

Miles	Timing point	Schedule	Class '5' 4-6-0s Nos 45371 and 45494 9 coaches (301/310 tons) Sunday 22 June 1958		Class '5' 4-6-0s Nos 45368 and 45451 10 coaches (334/345 tons) Sunday 6 July 1958	
6.30pm Keswick-Newcastle			Actual	Speed	Actual	Speed
0.0	KESWICK	0	0.00		0.00	
1.0	Briery Mill Halt		3.43	28	3.12	26
2.0	Milepost 15		5.39	33	5.22	28
3.0	Milepost 16		7.25	37	7.22	36
3.3	Stop for pilotman		8.28			
	Single line working		8.54			
3.5	Threlkeld	9	10.31	10	8.03	32
4.0	Milepost 17		12.48	24	9.12	27
4.5	Milepost 17½		13.54	28/31	10.17	26
5.0	Milepost 18		14.56	26	11.28	24
5.5	Milepost 18½		16.00	30	12.49	22
6.0	Milepost 19		17.05	27	14.04	24
6.5	Milepost 19½		18.09	28	15.16	25
7.0	Milepost 20		19.15	27	16.26	26
7.5	Milepost 20½		20.22	26	17.34	27
8.0	Milepost 21		21.30	27	18.42	27
8.2	Troutbeck		22.03	30	19.14	31
8.5	Milepost 21½		22.37	28	19.47	29
9.5	Milepost 22½		24.11	47	21.21	47
10.5	Penruddock	26	25.45	25/33	22.54	25/32
11.0	Milepost 24		26.47	32/50	23.51	33/48
12.0	Milepost 25		28.05	50	25.13	48
13.0	Flusco Sidings		29.13	59	26.21	62
14.4	Blencow	33	31.28	15	28.02	35
15.2	Catch points		32.43	45	29.02	48
16.6	Redhills Junction		34.21	63	30.36	65
					sigs	15
17.8	Penrith No 1		sig stops		32.52	
18.2	PENRITH	39	46.15		34.00	
	Net		34		33.50	

Logs courtesy of H. G. Ellison

disappeared, the strengthening to Keswick was mainly of value for the few heavy trains that travelled to and from Keswick, via Carlisle, principally the 'Newcastle' on summer Sundays. This train was usually worked by 'Black 5' 4-6-0s in pairs, or a '5MT' with a '5X',

or possibly even a three-cylinder 'Royal Scot' 4-6-0. No 46136 *The Border Regiment* was employed on Sundays 11 and 18 August and again on 1 September 1957 (see page 35). By courtesy of Mr Hugh G. Ellison, three logs of runs from Keswick are reproduced here.

Examples of the LMS family of large passenger tank engines also worked on the Keswick road in later years. This is Stanier 2-6-4T No 42594 climbing the gradient over Mosedale viaduct with 'The Lakes Express' of Saturday 19 August 1961. *Robert Leslie*

NER locomotives on the Keswick road

Reference has already been made to the accommodation of NER locomotives at Penrith (where a passenger engine for the Eden Valley line was housed) and Cockermouth (where provision of stabling was in fact never achieved). 'Day return' excursions from distant NER stations to Keswick have also been noted; six-coupled engines of, nominally, 'goods' classes are believed to have worked such trips, with perhaps an occasional 2-4-0 passenger engine, like those used on the Stainmore route.

The daily operation of NER locomotives, back to 1866, was on mineral duties. Until the first decade of the 20th century a near monopoly was held by the 'long boiler' 0-6-0s

of Stockton & Darlington Railway derivation, hence titled 'Quakers', collectively the '1001' Class. Broadly, their wheels were of 5-foot diameter, with inside cylinders (17 or 18in x 24in) and the weight of engine (not including tender) in working order was about 35 tons. 'Double loads' became normal by the 1880s-90s. Some 28 coke wagons, each of 10 tons capacity, and two brake-vans were worked by two 'Quakers'. This represented maybe 400 tons of train westbound, with one engine moved to the rear for the climb from Redhills Junction on the CKPR. Working from Shildon to Cockermouth and back in a single shift of 15-16 hours was typical, and a marathon undertaking for the men, taking in Stainmore (1,378 feet) and Troutbeck (889 feet) in both directions. As the length of the

Above This picture superbly illustrates the classic 'Quaker' long-boiler 0-6-0 engines of the S&DR/NER, for so long the motive power for the coke trains westward and (mainly) coke 'empties' returning to the County of Durham. No 1184 is pausing, eastbound, at Keswick, against Latrigg in the background. Note the comparatively light permanent way and the lack of trees near the station – and the panama hat! No 1184 was the locomotive involved in the westbound runaway early on 16 January 1896, when the signalman derailed it to avoid a collision. *D. F. Tee collection*

Below Kirkby Stephen shed provided most of the NER locomotives for the Cockermouth mineral trains, and 'Quaker' No 1177 is seen there, probably pre-1914. The electric lamp would be powered by the hydro-electric plant, which Kirkby Stephen stalwarts were always proud to show to visitors. *R. H. Inness collection, courtesy of the North Eastern Railway Association*

railwayman's working day was progressively curtailed, Kirkby Stephen became the normal staging point; thus Kirkby Stephen engines and their men worked from their home station to Cockermouth and back, turning their engine at the passenger station and taking a meal-time break while the traffic was dealt with at the lower yard.

From 1901 Wilson Worsdell of the NER designed and built the handsome 'T' and 'T1' 0-8-0 locomotives for mineral traffic, with 4ft 7¼in diameter wheels, outside cylinders (20in x 26in) and an engine-only weight in working order of rather more than 58 tons. In February 1904 he suggested to the CKPR that these new engines be employed on the NER's Cockermouth coke duties, by implication taking double loads unaided. CKPR General Manager Peter Thompson and Engineer John Wood visited Vincent Raven, Mr Worsdell's assistant, to learn more, but, as noted earlier, no agreement to strengthen bridges was achieved. The subject went into abeyance, although in August 1906 Mr Wood presented costs for the strengthening of bridges to take 'T' engines, but his Board elected not to proceed. The LNWR was rebuffed by the CKPR when, in May 1917, it wished to introduce heavier goods locomotives on the

line via Keswick, presumably visualising its own 0-8-0 engines.

Meanwhile, in July 1906, the CKPR agreed to accept the 'C' and 'C1' class 0-6-0 engines of the NER on their line. The 'C' was a two-cylinder compound locomotive and the 'C1' the non-compound version, with 5ft 1in diameter wheels (like the 'C') but with 18in x 24in cylinders and Joy's valve gear. The weight of the 'C1' engine in working order was about 41½ tons. This decision followed a meeting at Penrith between Messrs Thompson and Wood for the CKPR and Messrs Smeddle (District Locomotive Superintendent, Darlington) and Bengough (Civil Engineer) of the NER.

The true Wilson Worsdell 0-6-0 mineral engines were the 4ft 7¼in-wheeled 'P' (built 1894-98) and 'P1' (1899-1902), with 18in x 24in and 18¼in x 26in inside cylinders respectively. They had steam brakes on the engines but no continuous brake for the train, and in due time the 'C1' type (which also worked passenger trains on the NER) and the 'P' or 'P1' Classes (mineral-only engines) infiltrated the coke workings to Cockermouth.

An older class of 0-6-0, originating in the Fletcher period of locomotive design between

NER/LNER No 1133 of Fletcher's '398' Class is standing at Shildon, where the overhead conductor is seen for the 1500 volts DC electrified railway to Teesside. This class of engine also worked through to Cockermouth on the coke trains – from Shildon, Auckland or Kirkby Stephen sheds. *R. H. Inness, courtesy of Ken Hoole*

the S&DR 'Quakers' and the Worsdell types, was the '398' family, typically with 5-foot wheels, 17in x 24in cylinders and a weight of 35 tons; these engines came to be represented at Kirkby Stephen and shared the Cockermouth runs. An observer at Keswick in the summer of 1920 noted locomotives of 'C1' and '398' types, all identifiable with Kirkby Stephen shed, engaged on the coke duties. This was just about the end of the active years of coke traffic to Cockermouth.

The LNER employed Worsdell six-coupled locomotives on such traffic as survived into 1923-26 and 1928-29. It is not thought that the LNER, successors to the NER, ever worked passenger trains to Keswick with its own locomotives.

The CKPR's only locomotive

In the week when the CKPR opened its line to passenger traffic (5 January 1865), its Works Committee was authorised to purchase a small locomotive for use on the line if deemed necessary. On 11 May of that year the Committee asked the Engineer to secure quotations for the supply of a tank engine;

presumably the primary aim was to have a ballast engine, but the Secretary was to check with the LNWR that, if purchased, the locomotive could be employed occasionally in CKPR service. No doubt the LNWR was discouraging or worse, and the subject was dropped.

Coming to March 1900, the CKPR placed contracts for doubling the formation and structures of its route from Troutbeck to Penruddock and from Blencow to Redhills Junction; the contractor was W. Grisenthwaite of Penrith. The new lines were completed in June 1901, including laying of the extra tracks, accomplished under the arrangements of the railway company's own Engineer. *Contract Journal* of 26 June 1901 shows Manning Wardle locomotive Works No 1064 (an 0-6-0T) for sale by William Grisenthwaite, styled 'contractor'. The sale was handled by A. T. & E. Crow, who were well known as auctioneers of contract plant in the North of England. It was reported to the CKPR Board on 14 November 1901 that since their meeting on 10 October 1901, a locomotive engine, the property of Mr W.

This is the only locomotive ever owned by the CKPR, but was never permitted to work on the railway. It is seen here at Cockermouth. *LGRP*

Grisenthwaite, had been purchased at his plant sale, for the purpose of ballasting and repairs of the permanent way. It was resolved to purchase a suitable van to work with ballast trains and to erect a shed for the engine at Flusco Quarry, or other convenient place. One recalls later reference to 'the engine shed' at Flusco ballast quarry, thereby giving credence to this move.

The locomotive had inside cylinders (13in x 18in), 3-foot diameter wheels and a weight in working order of 22 tons. There was a raised round-top firebox and a large cab, with rounded eaves. It was one of the relatively few of Manning Wardle & Co's 'M' Class to be built with side tanks, and was maker's number 1064, dispatched new from the company's Leeds works in May 1888, with the name *Oldham*, to T. A. Walker, at Latchford. This was on the alignment of his linear contract between the Mersey estuary and Manchester Docks (to be), constructing the Manchester Ship Canal. Its disposal from the MSC job has not been recorded specifically, but would probably have occurred after the opening of the canal in 1894.

On coming to the CKPR the locomotive carried the name *Strachan No 7*. Contractors J. Strachan figure as owners in Mannings' records, but with no dates recorded. A likely place for its employment by them would have been on the construction of the LNWR Weaste branch (Eccles to the MSC Railway) in 1894-95. Subsequently Strachan made a new link line for the LYR between Whitehouse West and North Junctions; the contract was placed in October 1898 and the curved line opened in July 1900, with Strachan's locomotives for sale at nearby Penwortham Junction on 20 June 1900. Grisenthwaite could well have bought it here, to haul 'fill' on his CKPR project. A copy of the CKPR minutes of 14 November 1901 would go to Euston as a matter of course and in no time whatever a strong objection to the CKPR's new locomotive was on the desk of the General Manager at Keswick – from LNWR General Manager Frederick Harrison. Mr MacInnes, Carlisle Director of the LNWR and also a member of the CKPR Board, was asked to speak with Mr Harrison and set his

mind at rest. This was in vain and on 6 March 1902 Messrs Marshall, Glasson and Cropper (Charles James Cropper, of Burneside and a member of LNWR and CKPR Boards) met with – or were arraigned before (!) – LNWR Chairman Lord Stalbridge and Frederick Harrison, at Euston, to discuss *Strachan No 7*. The LNWR officers viewed this as a matter of principle at stake; it was agreed that the LNWR would supply engine power as and when required by the CKPR for maintenance of its permanent way, or like needs. It transpired that the CKPR had used NER engines for such purposes, for the provision of which they paid, but the practice had ceased 'for a long time'.

The Keswick Board resolved on 8 May 1902 to sell their locomotive, 'as soon as a favourable opportunity offers'. Three years later, Mr Cropper drew attention to the locomotive still being unsold and the Directors reiterated their wish to sell – at over £300. The topic next figured in the Board room some eight years later, on 5 July 1913, when the Secretary reported: 'The Company's locomotive engine, which has stood for some time in the carriage shed at Cockermouth passenger station, has been sold for £100.' Unfortunately the purchaser was not named, but a short account in *The Locomotive* of 15 May 1926 states that it was sold in June 1913 (which reconciles) to Mr Isaac Miller, of Carlisle. The 1913 directories show only R. Miller, 'old iron merchant', of 15a John Street, but one Isaac Miller, machinery merchant, of the Currock district, advertised locomotives for sale in the early 1920s.

William Firth (maybe of William Firth Ltd, Doncaster, who advertised engines for sale or hire in 1913-14) sold Manning Wardle No 1064 around November 1914 to Hudswell Clarke of Leeds (across the street from their contemporaries, Manning Wardle). After repairs it was resold by HC to Sir John Jackson, a public works contractor, and sent to Codford (between Salisbury and Westbury), named *Prince Edward*. Jacksons' relevant bills were paid by the War Department ('Secretary of State for War' in Manning Wardle records), which thus acquired the locomotive. The last supply of spare parts by Manning Wardle was dated 26 February 1917. The correspondents of *The Locomotive* did not mention Codford, but believed that the engine later worked in Galloway, south-west Scotland, so perhaps that was also an assignment for the War Department.

The late Syd Ridley (who used to live at Motherby, and was the last known 'servant' of the CKPR, with a lively memory) vividly recalled that, around 1912-13 (when he would be seven or eight years old), he sometimes visited his elder brother, then employed at Cockermouth station. Syd and another boy liked to explore the recesses of the M&CR carriage shed, where they would mount and 'drive' a stored locomotive called *Strachan*. Mr Ridley associated it with the dozen (stated) ballast wagons of the CKPR, which had wooden 'dumb' buffers. Incidentally, an addition of four vehicles to the company's ballast wagon fleet had been authorised in 1892, and in July 1913 there was a proposal to adapt one or two of the wagons for use at the vehicle loading bank at Keswick. It is believed that the ballast train wagons used in the later days of the CKPR were LNWR vehicles. Mr Ridley understood that *Strachan* had been bought from a Scottish colliery and eventually went back to Scotland; this could derive from the Strachan firm's origins and, subsequently, might associate with Galloway.

The information in this section derives mainly from: Syd Ridley; T. H. Braithwaite (of Workington) and F. Stanley (an accountant of the CKPR section of the LMS) published in *The Locomotive* of 15 May 1926 (refer also to 15 June 1926); J. B. Latham; Russell Wear; the records of Manning Wardle and Hudswell Clarke, of Leeds; the photograph of the locomotive reproduced by W. McGowan Gradon and later listed by LGRP as No 12726 (reproduced here); and the Board minutes of the CKPR.

8. Senior and specialist staff

C&WR staff

Samuel Harford, station master at Masboro (Rotherham), Midland Railway, was appointed Secretary of the C&WR but died on 24 March 1845, before he was due to move to Cockermouth. George H. Barnes, from the London, Brighton & South Coast Railway, was subsequently appointed in August 1845, but moved on in November 1846 to become Secretary of the M&CR. His successor was Henry Jacob, from the East Lancashire Extension Railway (the line from near Ramsbottom to Colne), and he was styled Secretary & General Superintendent of the C&WR. Within a few years the chief officer was John Dodds, who served until his resignation wef 12 August 1856, being by then 'Secretary, Engineer and Manager'. One gains the impression that he was latterly unpopular with his Board, but he moved to Edinburgh and continued for a time to take a critical interest in the affairs of the Cockermouth company. Mr Tosh was temporarily Manager and Superintendent, and, at the Board's request, he prepared an urgent report on the run-down condition of the locomotives. John Mayson was Secretary from August 1856 and shortly became Secretary & General Manager – appointments held for some ten years. Mr Tosh figured as Locomotive Superintendent and Thomas Drane, CE, was for a number of years the (Civil) Engineer.

John Mayson was placed in charge of the LNWR's 'Whitehaven District' following its creation in 1866-67 from the acquired Whitehaven Junction and Cockermouth & Workington Railways; he was (or soon became) 'District Manager'. He adopted the name 'J. Myson' to avoid confusion with Masons on the LNWR, but resigned around August 1869. G. P. Neele wrote, much later, that Mr Mayson's career with the LNWR was short and unsuccessful.

CKPR staff

The chief officer of the company was the **Secretary & Manager (Secretary & General Manager** from 1870); there were effectively only three successive incumbents from 1861 to 1923. Henry Cattle was appointed on 10 August 1861 at the first Board meeting. He had been chief clerk to A. C. Sheriff in the Hull District of the York & North Midland Railway. In 1864 he became the first representative of the CKPR with the Railway Clearing House. He resigned in July 1870, moving to the Cambrian Railways' headquarters at Oswestry as their General Manager – or so it was understood in Keswick, although 'traffic manager' may have been more accurate. At least two of his best men soon followed him from Keswick.

Peter Thompson, previously the company's Accountant, was appointed on 21 July 1870 and held the senior office on the CKPR until resigning on 1 March 1913 to take a seat on the company Board.

John Clark, Traffic Superintendent, appears to have carried out all or most of the duties of Secretary & General Manager in 1913-14 and was formally appointed as such from 1 July 1914; he carried these responsibilities until the winding up of the company in 1923. There had been a somewhat mysterious interregnum before John Clark was appointed. In anticipation of Peter Thompson's resignation, the office of Secretary & General Manager seems to have been advertised and A. Entwistle was appointed wef 1 March 1913. A personal letter from Mr Entwistle, of 39 Dorset Square (near Marylebone station), London, to a Director of the CKPR was dated 25 February 1913 and expressed pleasure that the appointment would bring him back to old families and friends. There may be an implication that he had served the CKPR earlier in his career. Both the company and personal files, so far as they exist, are silent until the minuting on 4 July 1914 that Mr Entwistle had withdrawn his acceptance of office.

As mentioned above, Peter Thompson was CKPR **Accountant** until 1870 and he may well earlier have been the inspector of permanent way and mineral traffic engaged by the C&WR in August 1856. In 1870 he was succeeded as Accountant by Joseph Wales, previously station master at Cockermouth. An unhappy story ended in July 1885 with talk of criminal proceedings after defalcations

Peter Thompson probably joined the Cockermouth & Workington Railway in 1856. He progressed rapidly to be Secretary & General Manager of the Cockermouth, Keswick & Penrith Railway, from 1870 until1913, and a Director from 1913 until his death in 1920. *Richard L. Pattinson/CRA*

This letter from Peter Thompson, written (to Mr James Irving, Share Broker, Carlisle) soon after he became Secretary & General Manager of the CKPR, reads: 'Dear Sir, I enclose share transfer certificate of forty £4 shares from the Cumberland Union Banking Co to Charles Rowe. I have received the Company's fee 2/6. Yours truly, P. Thompson.' *Courtesy of Derek Brough*

of some £1,388 had allegedly been found in the company's accounts.

John Postlethwaite, who had been Storekeeper & Chief Clerk, was made Accountant in May 1886, and resigned owing to poor health in June 1914. He was placed on pension and was among the people granted a gratuity in 1923. F. Stanley held the appointment from 1914 to 1923.

The first **Traffic Superintendent** was John Clark, who had been Chief Clerk in the Secretary's office from at least 1870 until 1886, when 'traffic' was added to his responsibilities – and in due course he was 'Traffic Superintendent', promoted in July 1914 to be the chief officer of the Company.

John Robinson, previously cashier, was Traffic Superintendent from 1 July 1914 until 1923.

The appointment of Thomas Bouch as **Engineer** was made at the first Board meeting, on 10 August 1861, and he had overall responsibility for survey, design and construction of the railway and all its works. John Wood (CE by 1869; MInstCE by 1880) was resident engineer during construction (1862-64) and he was formally appointed Engineer of the company by the Works Committee on 6 October 1864, confirmed by the Board on 5 January 1865, this appointment to be fully effective 'when his arrangement with Mr Bouch terminates'. John Wood was allowed private practice and he had a Carlisle address during many of his years with the CKPR. The doubling of sections of the line and the remodelling of Keswick station came within his province, regarding survey, design and execution. He was rewarded by significant gratuities on completion of these projects; note that the company had been saved the engagement of a consulting engineer. When John Wood retired in November 1905, unanimous appreciation was expressed by Board members, including that 'for ready assistance ever given in all circumstances of emergency and his soundness and wisdom in counsel on all occasions.' In 1908 they invited him to join the Board, but he declined on health grounds.

A. M. Bristow was Engineer from 1 December 1905 until August 1920, when he retired owing to poor health but was retained on inside work; he died on 23 October 1922. J. C. Boyd CE held the appointment from 1 September 1920; he did not receive a gratuity in 1923, so perhaps he had moved to an appointment elsewhere towards that time.

The gratuities of 10 March 1923, approved by the LMS, ranged from £1,000 to £30 and went to John Clark and other serving officers, senior head office clerks, station masters, the permanent way inspector and the former Accountant.

Other appointments in CKPR days included those of cashier, storekeeper, chief clerks and other clerks at Keswick head office, booking clerk at Keswick, and goods clerk/agent at Keswick. Notable among the latter was Percy Sanderson, who joined the old company in 1911 and served both the LMS and BR at Keswick until 1958, in which time he also worked on behalf of staff and for the community as councillor and mayor. There was also the warehouseman at Keswick, the signal fitter and his assistant (G. W. Carlton and Edward Elliott in 1913), a telegraph lineman and assistant, blacksmith, mason, joiner (R. Nichol in 1913), fencer (Nathan Routledge, c1913-23), gardener (James Shrives, mentioned elsewhere), foreman of the labourers' gang, a timber loader and assistant with roving commission, and the policemen.

The Inspector of Permanent Way was a significant figure especially during the doubling works from the 1890s to 1902, and each track gang had its own foreman ganger and platelayers, with their 'length' to watch and maintain. The staff at Cockermouth were joint staff of the CKPR and C&WR, and from 1866 to 1923 of the CKPR and LNWR.

The C&WR Board of Directors

The company was formed by Act of Parliament of 21 July 1845. Its initial Board of 12 members was elected on 15 August of that year; the members in question were still on the Board in June 1847, a couple of months after the line opened. The following record may omit some members of short tenure; it is not claimed as definitive in identifying the members of the Harris family, who, with the Fletchers, were prominent in Cumberland coalmining.

John Wilson Fletcher of Tarn Bank, Greysouthen, had been on the provisional committee formed on 26 July 1844 and was Chairman of the company from 15 August 1845; he was a member of Board (and its Chairman) for many of the following years until his death in October 1857.

Joseph Harris of Lorton was on the provisional committee, but it is unclear whether he was on the Board for a time.

Joseph Harris of Greysouthen (sometimes described as of Brigham) was on the provisional committee, and on the Board as Deputy Chairman from 15 August 1845 until 1855. He would be the coalowner, of

This group of railwaymen, seen at Troutbeck in CKPR days, comprises Richard Hebson (left) and Joseph Watson (right), at the time senior and second signalmen, and Tom Mitchinson (seated, right), the ganger in charge of the length. His colleagues of the gang are Mark Cockbain (seated, left), Chapelhow and William Bainbridge (standing, second and third from the left) and T. Thwaite (the tall figure), the assistant timber loader, who moved to Australia. James Postlethwaite, the CKPR's timber loader, took the photograph. Dick Hebson has 'CKP' tabs on his jacket collar. Joe Watson and T. Thwaite are wearing the CKPR company's green corduroy uniform. *Courtesy of Ted Watson*

The staff at Cockermouth station are gathered in the entrance. A proclamation is glimpsed beyond, perhaps the Armistice of 1918 – significantly, a member of staff killed in this war does not appear. The folk shown are: (standing, L-R) an unidentified tall figure wearing traditional CKPR jacket and green corduroy trousers, and prominent 'CJS' (Cockermouth Joint Station) lapel badges; an S&T inspector (with bowler); T. Armstrong (porter, from 1901); John Vickers (in service since 1900); Robert Little (station master, 1891-1921); a tall porter; Mark Allinson (signalman); Thomas Arthur Ridley (elder brother of Syd); and Jack Stanley (signalman). Kneeling (L-R) are: son of Reg Litt; Reg Litt; Billy Hartley; and Percy Sanderson (clerk). *Courtesy of Syd Ridley Jnr*

Uniform buttons in brass carry the monograms 'CKPR' and 'CJS' (Cockermouth Joint Station). Also illustrated are buttons from the LMS and BR (the LMS in silver finish, the BR in aluminium/silver) and LNER. Note the unusual 'LMS & LNE' button, a style that suggests very early days after the 1923 railway Grouping and possibly worn by Penrith station staff. *From the collection of the late Syd Ridley, by courtesy of Mrs Ridley*

J. M. Cutts, station master at Troutbeck, 1912-c1926, is seen at his station in the CKPR era, wearing the company's dignified attire for its station masters. The raised letters 'CK&PR' appear on his hat, just below the brim. Note also the whistle. A 'buttonhole' is worn – and the bar and cross of the St John Ambulance Association. It was Mr Cutts who first established a Sunday service in a room at Troutbeck station, a similar arrangement later being facilitated in a room on the down side by Mr Cecil Oldfield, when he was station master at Threlkeld and Troutbeck. *Courtesy of Ted Watson*

Greysouthen Colliery, who died on 7 January 1860.

Jonathan Harris, Jnr CE was on the company Board from 15 August 1845 and probably throughout until his death, including a spell as Chairman c1853-56. This would be Capt John Harris CE, who succeeded as principal of Greysouthen Collieries and Brigham Limeworks and estates in January 1860. He died on 25 January 1863. Many of the family's industrial interests were thereafter acquired by the Fletchers and so reached the West Cumberland Hematite I & S Co Ltd and the Allerdale Coal Company.

Joseph William Harris, probably of Papcastle, was a member of the provisional committee but not the company Board until its later years; he was certainly a member from 1856 to 1866. He is thought to be of W. Harris & Sons, the textile interests of the family, in Cockermouth.

John Charlton of Workington served on the Board from 15 August 1845 until about 1857.

George Cape of Cockermouth was a member of the provisional committee and also the Board from 15 August 1845 until at least 1859. He provided office furniture in 1846 and looked after the brickwork of the foundations for Cockermouth station in 1856. In June 1857 he complained to the Secretary that he had visited the office and found no clerks present!

John Mordy and **Abraham Robinson** were both elected to the board on 15 August 1845 and served through to 1847, but ceased to be members after the early years.

John Steel of Derwent Bank, Cockermouth, served on the provisional committee and was a member of the Board from 15 August 1845 through to the LNWR take-over in 1866. He was Chairman from 17 November 1857, following the late J. W. Fletcher. He was also the company's solicitor, although not in his days as Chairman.

William Thornburn of Papcastle was a member of the provisional committee and served the company Board from 15 August 1845 until retirement on 31 July 1856. He figured as a coalowner, shipping coals by way of the C&WR and Workington Harbour. (Note also Wm Thornburn, Jnr, below.)

Thomas Westray of Kendal (later of Workington) was on the Board from 15 August 1845 and in its early days. He resumed a seat in 1852 until retirement in July 1857.

John Whitwell of Kendal, presumed to be the brewer, was a member of the Board from 15 August 1845 until 1852.

Jonathan Wood of Cockermouth was on the provisional committee and on the Board from 15 August 1845 until retirement on 31 July 1856.

Isaac Fisher of Seaton joined the Board in its early years but was not a member by the 1860-64 period.

George Castle of Hensingham, Whitehaven, joined the Board in its early years and was a member until his death in about December 1856.

W. Wood joined in about 1854 but dropped out by 1855-57.

Rev Samuel Sherwin of Dean probably joined the Board in 1855-56 and attended a general meeting on 31 January 1857; he attended no Board meetings in 1856-57 and resigned in July 1857.

Edward Waugh of Papcastle was Deputy Chairman of the company in 1856-66 and continued as solicitor in succession to John Steel, through to the LNWR take-over. He was a promoter of the CKPR and for a long period its solicitor.

William Kitchen of Whitehaven joined the Board on 31 July 1856 but resigned in July 1857. However, he (or a son of the same name and town?) joined the Board on 17 November 1857 – but then dropped out in the period 1860-64.

William Thornburn, Jnr of Papcastle joined the Board on 31 July 1856, in succession to William Thornburn, Snr. He resigned in June 1863, being then resident in London.

Henry Fletcher of Marsh Side, Workington, joined the Board on 16 December 1856 and continued until 1866. He is believed to be a son of J. W. Fletcher, who died in October 1857 as Chairman of the C&WR.

John Musgrave of Whitehaven joined the Board on 22 July 1857 and continued until 1866. He was a solicitor.

Isaac Fletcher of Tarn Bank, Greysouthen, joined the Board on 17 November 1857, succeeding his late father J. W. Fletcher. He served until resigning on 24 February 1863. He was appointed Chairman of the CKPR in 1867 and was MP for Cockermouth from 1868 to 1879, as well as a Director of the West Cumberland Hematite I & S Co Ltd.

William Fletcher of Brigham Hill, Brigham, joined the Board on 24 February 1863 and continued in office until 1866. He was a son of the late J. W. Fletcher and brother of Isaac Fletcher (*ante*). He was appointed in August 1864 to the Cockermouth Joint Station Committee. He was a Director of the CKPR from its inception. He followed his brother as MP for Cockermouth (1879-80) and was Chairman of the Cockermouth & Workington Junction Railway from 1880 to 1900. Later he was Managing Director of the Allerdale Coal Company and also established the Moresby Coal Company.

Isaac Gray Bass of The Crags, Broughton, joined the Board in about August 1861 and continued as a member until 1866.

James Dees of Whitehaven joined the Board around August 1863 and remained a member until 1866. He also served as Engineer of the M&CR (1850-59), Engineer to the Whitehaven Junction Railway by 1852 and until 1856, and Engineer of the WC&ER (1854-57). One notes also his report on the C&WR line and its timber bridges in later 1856.

Robert Gibson of Whitehaven joined the Board in about September 1863 and continued as a member until 1866.

Note: The nine members listed as continuing until 1866 relinquished their office on the transfer of the company to the LNWR.

The CKPR Board of Directors

The company was incorporated by an Act of 1 August 1861. When the first formal meeting of the company was held on 10 August 1861, at the Royal Oak, Keswick, the existing 'provisional committee' was superseded by a constituted Board of 12 members (15 from 31 August 1861). T. A. Hoskins was Chairman and Isaac Fletcher Deputy Chairman. Following the agreements negotiated with the LNWR and the S&DR during February-September 1862, seven members (whose names were obtained by ballot) resigned their seats on 28 February 1863 and two nominees of the LNWR were elected shortly after this.

The way was thus paved for a Board of 12 members, eight locally nominated, two nominated by the LNWR and two by the S&DR/NER – a pattern that continued to the Grouping of 1923, when the company passed out of existence, being absorbed into the newly created London Midland & Scottish Railway Company. The seven members who resigned on 28 February 1863 were John Crozier, Arthur Dover, Isaac Gale and John Robinson (all elected 10 August 1861), and Mark Cockbaine, William Fletcher and John Steel, MP (all elected 31 August 1861).

The following table shows the eight 'survivors' of February 1863, followed by the four appointees of the larger companies, then subsequent other appointments down the years. Where members are designated with military rank, or as JP or MP, this does not necessarily apply throughout the period of Directorship. Dates of joining or leaving the board, where shown in month and year only, are to be taken as approximate.

Miles MacInnes (1830-1909) of Carlisle, a thoughtful participant in Board deliberations at Euston, is seen as sketched by a fellow Director of the LNWR, some six months before his death. He joined the LNWR and CKPR Boards in 1876 and was greatly respected and liked by colleagues and staff.
Courtesy of Gurney MacInnes

Board members, Cockermouth, Keswick & Penrith Railway

Date joined	Name, rank/appointments and address	Company duties/other interests	Left Board
10.8.1861	Thomas Alison Hoskins, JP. Higham Hall (near Bassenthwaite Lake station)	Chairman 28.2.1863-2.11.1867; 'turned first sod' 21.5.1862.	Retired 2.11.1867
10.8.1861	Isaac Fletcher, JP (1827-79); MP for Cockermouth; elder son of John Wilson Fletcher, former C&WR Chairman. Tarn Bank, Greysouthen	Deputy Chairman 28.2.1863-1.11.1867. Chairman 2.11.1867 until c4.1879. Also first Chairman of Keswick Hotel Co. Partner in family coal-owners Isaac & William Fletcher & Co.	Died 4.1879
10.8.1861	Isaac Gray Bass. The Crags, Broughton (north of River Derwent)	Interested in coal and iron. When tendering resignation, wrote from Aston Hall Colliery, Hawarden (noted for early tramway); was about to move from Cumberland.	Retired 26.4.1867
10.8.1861	John Jameson, JP. Moorhouses, Penrith	Deputy Chairman from 2.11.1867. Chairman from 4.1879 (but again Deputy from 9.1879, at his wish).	Died 10.1881
10.8.1861	Isaac Lowthian. Penrith; Chatsworth Square, Carlisle, by 1879	Resignation due to continued ill health.	Retired 4.2.1880
10.8.1861	Thomas McGlasson. Penrith	Of Penrith brewers	Died 8.1870
10.8.1861	John Simpson. Penrith		Died 7.1872
10.8.1861	John James Spedding, Major JP. Greta Bank, Keswick, with lands above the station; later of Windebrowe	Deputy Chairman from 11.6.1879. Chairman from 6.8.1879. Pulpit in Crosthwaite Church, Keswick, is a memorial to him.	Died 8.12.1909

Date	Name and details	Notes	Died/Retired
28.3.1863	William Nicholson Hodgson, DL JP; MP for Carlisle/East Cumberland (ranging 1847-76). Newby Grange, Crosby, Carlisle (and 33 Duke Street, St James's, London)	Nominee of LNWR	Died 11.1876
28.3.1863	Andrew Green Thompson, Major (later Colonel) JP. The Hollies, Keswick (also of Bridekirk, near Cockermouth)	Nominee of LNWR. Interested in W Cumberland iron and steel industry.	Retired (?) 1882
25.4.1863	Henry Pease, MP. Pierremont, Darlington	Nominee of S&DR/NER and Chairman of S&DR; Director of NER, Tees Valley Rly, Eden Valley Rly, SDLUR	Died 8.1881
25.4.1863	Isaac Wilson, JP. Nunthorpe Hall, Middlesbrough	Nominee of S&DR/NER and Director of S&DR/NER, EVR, SDLUR, etc; a figure in the Teesside iron industry.	Retired 8.1879
11.5.1867	Henry Gandy, Capt DL JP; son of John Gandy, of Oakland, Windermere; became High Sheriff of Westmorland. Eden Grove, Penrith; Castle Bank, Appleby; Skirgill Park, Penrith (bought 1879, sold by his son in 1925)		Died 6.1888
2.11.1867	Arthur Dover. Skiddaw Bank, Keswick	Also a Board member 1861-63.	Died 1.1874
c8.1870	C. H. Wake, Lt-Col. Ormathwaite House, Keswick		Died 2.1872
24.2.1872	Hon Percy S. Wyndham, MP. Cockermouth Castle/Isell Hall (Leconfield Estates)	An infrequent attendee at Board meetings.	Retired 6.1876

Date joined	Name, rank/appointments and address	Company duties/other interests	
27.7.1872	William Harrison. Penrith		Died 6.1878
7.2.1874	William McGlasson. The Close, Embleton	Farmer and landowner. Brother of Thomas who died 1870 (*ante*)	Died 7.1890
14.6.1876	Henry Charles Howard, DL BA JP (1850-1914); High Sheriff of Cumberland 1879, MP for Penrith 1885-86. Greystoke Castle (inherited Greystoke estates but not the associated Dukedom)	Deputy Chairman from 8.11.1906; Chairman from 13.1.1910.	Died 8.1914
29.11.1876	Miles MacInnes, BA MA JP (1830-1909); eldest son of Gen John MacInnes (d1859) of Fern Lodge, Hampstead; became Alderman and Vice Chairman of Cumberland CC, and Deputy Lt; MP (Lib) for Hexham 1885-95. West Heath, Hampstead, but soon moved to Rickerby House, Carlisle (to which he succeeded in 1876 under will of George Head Head, of Head's Bank, Carlisle), which remained in family until 1914.	Joined LNWR Board and (as LNWR nominee) CKPR Board simultaneously in 1876, as successor to W. N. Hodgson, also of Carlisle. On his death, Secretary of LNWR Temperance Union, Carlisle, wrote: 'We have lost our very best friend, on whom railwaymen on the LNWR line have looked for help when in trouble and also in our Christian and temperance work.' 'George the Fifth' Class 4-4-0 No 2507 (LNWR)/5335 (LMS) named *Miles MacInnes* 1910-35.	Died 10.1909
7.8.1878	Sir Henry Ralph Fletcher-Vane, Bart DL JP (1830-1908). Hutton-in-the-Forest. (From 1964 William Morgan Fletcher-Vane was created Baron Inglewood)	Deputy Chairman 27.8.1881-4.10.1906, but remained on Board thereafter.	Died 6.1908
11.6.1879	Edward Waugh, MP (from 8.1881). Cockermouth	A prominent figure in the town, he had been on the C&WR Board and a promoter of the CKPR. Served the CKPR as solicitor from its formation until 6.1879 (when Edward Lamb Waugh was appointed).	Died 3.1891

Date	Name / Address	Notes	Status
8.1879	Alfred Kitching. Elmfield, Darlington	Nominee of NER. Presumed to be Alfred Kitching (1808-82), partner in William & Alfred Kitching of Hope Town Foundry, Darlington (cf locos built 1846-47 for C&WR).	Died 13.2.1882
14.2.1880	Thomas Altham. Penrith	Cf the foundry and ironmongery business of Penrith in 1880s, and indeed in 1980s.	Died 14.8.1900
19.8.1881	David Dale (becoming Sir David Dale, Bart). West Lodge, Darlington	Nominee of NER, with S&DR and Consett Iron Co links.	Died 4.1906
5.10.1881	John Pattinson. Vale View, St Bees; Greenbank, Whitehaven	Principal of the family flour mills, adjoining Whitehaven harbour and Bransty station (see also J. W. Pattinson below).	Died 3.1903
9.8.1882	James Cropper; MP for Kendal for 15 years and Chairman of Westmorland CC from 1888. Ellergreen, Burneside, Kendal	Nominee of LNWR. Principal of James Cropper & Co, paper mills, Burneside (see also Charles James Cropper below).	Died 16.10.1900
1882	Sir Henry M. Meysey-Thompson, Bart MP (later Lord Knaresborough). Kirkby Hall, York	Nominee of NER. Very infrequent attendee. Note that his father, Sir Harry S. Meysey-Thompson, Bart, had been Chairman of YNMR 1849-54 and on NER Board 1855-74.	Retired 5.1901
11.7.1888	Reginald Dykes Marshall, DL JP (1832-1913); grandson of John Marshall, of Patterdale Hall; son of John Marshall (1797-1836), MP for Leeds, who purchased the family estates near Derwentwater in 1832 and put in hand building of St John's Church, Keswick. Castlerigg Manor, Keswick	Very active Director 1888-1913. Deputy Chairman from 13.1.1910.	Died 10.1913

Date joined	Name, rank/appointments and address	Company duties/other interests	
9.8.1890	Thomas Glasson (of McGlasson family); son of Thomas (d1870, *ante*). Castle Bank, Penrith (later quoted as Barco, Penrith)	Penrith brewer, also (by 1910-11) Chairman of Threlkeld Granite Co. CKPR passed through his lands in the Redhills-Stainton vicinity.	Died 7.1912
9.5.1891	Hamlet Riley, Major DL LLB JP (1851-1922); High Sheriff of Cumberland, 1901. Ennim, Blencow	Deputy Chairman from 12.1913; Chairman from 8.1914.	Died 14.10.1922
25.8.1900	John Watson Nelson. Eden Bank, Langwathby		Died 9.1913
16.11.1900	Charles James Cropper. Ellergreen, Burneside, Kendal	Nominee of LNWR on death of James Cropper. Chairman of James Cropper & Co Ltd. 'Claughton' Class 4-6-0 No 1567 (LNWR)/5917 (LMS), one of the LNWR's premier express locos, named *Charles J. Cropper* 1914-34.	3.1923
17.5.1901	Hon Cecil Duncombe (of the Fevershams, of Duncombe Park, Helmsley). Newton Grange, York	Nominee of NER. Attended a Keswick Board meeting on 11.7.1901 but seemingly no others.	Died 20.5.1902
1.8.1902	Harry Tennant (sometimes Henry, as beneath his portrait in NER Boardroom). Holgate Hill House, York	Nominee of NER. On NER Board 1891-1910 and Deputy Chairman of NER 1905-10. Attended at Keswick 30.8.1902, then not until 12.4.1906 (when there was a NER item on the Board agenda).	Died 10.1910
14.5.1903	John William Pattinson (1871-1931). Richmond Hill, Whitehaven (to 1914); Bolton Hall, Gosforth (1914-19); Ravenstone, Bassenthwaite (1919-26)	Principal of the millers at Whitehaven. Followed his father John on the CKPR Board and was a regular attendee. Chairman from 11.1922. Other directorial interests included Threlkeld Granite Co Ltd and at one time the Keswick Hotel Co.	3.1923

Date	Name and details	Notes	End date
28.5.1906	Arthur Francis Pease. Hummersknott, Darlington	Nominee of NER. Believed never to have attended at Keswick Board meetings.	Retired 6.1907
12.7.1907	Edmund Russborough Turton, MP. Upsall Castle, Thirsk	Nominee of NER. Attended at Keswick 31.8.1907, then intermittently. Served as Chairman of RCH in addition to NER and other railway company directorships.	3.1923
13.8.1908	Christopher John Parker, DL JP (1859-1932). The Laithes, Skelton, Penrith (a property that he bought); other Parker family houses and estates in Penrith and CKPR territory included Lattendales at Greystoke, now well known as a Quaker guest house.	Deputy Chairman from 1922.	3.1923
3.2.1910	Frederick William Chance, later Sir F. W. Chance, KBE (1852-1932); MP for Carlisle 1905-09, Mayor 1907 and High Sheriff of Cumberland 1915. Morton, Carlisle.	Nominee of LNWR. From a notable family in Carlisle and district, he was a Director of Ferguson Brothers, cotton manufacturers, of Holme Head, Carlisle.	3.1923
10.2.1910	John S. Randles (1857-1945); knighted 1913; MP (Con) for Cockermouth 1900-06 and 1906-10, Manchester NW 1912-18, and Manchester Exchange 1918-22; son of Rev Marshall Randles DD (1826-1904), Professor of Theology at Wesleyan college, Didsbury; Sir John and Lady Randles (née Elia Hartley Spencer) spent the winter of 1913-14 in India, where he addressed Wesleyan missions. Bristowe Hill, Keswick.	Joined Board of Moss Bay HI & S Co Ltd in 1890 and became Chairman of Workington I & S Co Ltd on its formation in 1909. Also a Director of FR, 1911-23.	3.1923

Date joined	Name, rank/appointments and address	Company duties/other interests	
13.10.1910	Sir Walter Richard Plummer; member of Cumberland CC. 4 Queen's Square, Newcastle-upon-Tyne	Nominee of NER. Attended occasionally at Keswick.	Died 10.12.1917
1.3.1913	Peter Thompson. Mellan, Keswick	On staff of CKPR before opening in 1865; Secretary and Manager from 21.7.1870. Gave up these offices in 1913 to join the Board.	Died 29.8.1920
6.12.1913	Robert Jackson Holdsworth. 110 Chorley New Road, Bolton; Seat How(e), Thornthwaite, from 1925 – of Wood End, Thornthwaite	Cotton spinner, thus having Bolton associations. Also a Director of Cumberland Granite Co, of Embleton, and later of Keswick Granite Co Ltd.	3.1923
6.12.1913	Thomas William Mark. Great Crosthwaite, Keswick		3.1923
7.11.1914	Robert Ernest Highton (1858-1931); Mayor of Workington 1902-05 and 1910-14, and a Cumberland County Councillor. Newlands, Workington; Threlkeld Leys, nr Cockermouth	General Manager of Moss Bay HI & S Co Ltd, with other interests in iron and steel.	3.1923
2.1918	Hon C. W. Lowther, Major MP; son of James Lowther, first Lord Ullswater. 14 Wilton Street, London SW1; Westwood, Mayfield, Sussex	Nominee of NER	3.1923

Cockermouth, Keswick and Penrith Railway.

SECRETARY'S OFFICE,

KESWICK,

March 2nd, 1923.

We beg to inform you that a SPECIAL GENERAL MEETING of the Proprietors and the Debenture Stock-holders of the COCKERMOUTH, KESWICK & PENRITH RAILWAY COMPANY will, in accordance with the Railways Act, 1921, be held at the Keswick Hotel, Keswick, on Saturday, the 17th day of March, 1923, at 11-0 a.m. precisely, for the purpose of considering and, if so determined, of approving a preliminary Scheme in pursuance of the said Act for the absorption of the Cockermouth, Keswick & Penrith Railway Company by the London Midland & Scottish Railway Company.

We beg to forward you herewith a blank form of Proxy, with instructions for the use of the same in the event of your being unable to attend the Meeting, and if you desire to make use of the Proxy, a penny stamp must be affixed thereto previously to its being signed, and the Proxy, when filled up and signed, must be transmitted to the Secretary so that he may receive it not later than forty-eight hours before the time appointed for holding the Meeting.

JOHN WILLIAM PATTINSON, *Chairman.*

JOHN CLARK, *Secretary.*

A special general meeting of the CKPR was held on 17 March 1923 to formalise the company's absorption into the London Midland & Scottish Railway, at the Grouping of 1 January 1923. This was the letter sent to shareholders. *Harold D. Bowtell collection*

The last meeting of the Directors and officials of the Cockermouth, Keswick & Penrith Railway was held on 24 March 1923. The group is shown outside the Keswick Hotel. Sitting (L-R) are: Edmund Russborough Turton MP, Upsall Castle, near Thirsk (Director), nominated by the NER; Christopher John Parker MFH JP, The Laithes, near Penrith (Deputy Chairman); John William Pattinson JP, Ravenstone, near Keswick (Chairman); John Clark (Secretary & General Manager); Sir John Scurrah Randles MP, Bristowe Hill, Keswick (Director). Standing (L-R) are: F. Stanley (Accountant); The Hon Christopher W. Lowther MP, 14 Wilton Street, London, SW1 (Director), nominated by the NER; Robert Jackson Holdsworth, Seat How, Thornthwaite, near Keswick (Director); J. C. Boyd (Engineer); Robert Ernest Highton JP CC, Threlkeld Leys, near Cockermouth (Director); Charles James Cropper, Ellergreen, near Kendal (Director), nominated by the LNWR; Thomas William Mark, Great Crosthwaite, Keswick (Director); Charles Hugh Pattinson, The Towers, Cockermouth (Auditor); and J. Robinson (Traffic Superintendent).

The equanimity of the members of the Board was threatened in February 1913, when, at the shareholders' meeting, there was apparently an attempt not to re-elect Christopher Parker, of Penrith, a member since 1908. However, at an adjourned meeting on 29 March 1913 he was re-appointed by a majority of 673 votes (perhaps implying that shares counted as votes) – and he continued as a member right through to the last meeting, on 24 March 1923. Also in February 1913, John Randles, of Keswick, confided to J. W. Pattinson that, 'Mr Mark is very determined to clear Howard out and says that Howard ought to come home and fight.' Henry C. Howard, of Greystoke Castle, had been a Board member for 37 years and was Chairman of the company. Doubtless the reference is to Thomas W. Mark, of Keswick, presumably an influential shareholder who felt strongly that the Chairman was ineffective. In the event, T. W. Mark was himself elected to the Board in December of that year (1913) and Henry Howard died in August 1914, still as Chairman, to be succeeded by Major Hamlet Riley. Mr Mark served until 1923.

From the time of completion of the station buildings at Keswick, in the early days of the CKPR company, Board meetings were held in the Board room. On 24 March 1923 the final meeting was attended by eight members, namely six local directors and the two NER nominees. The two members who died in 1920 and 1922 had not been replaced and the two LNWR nominees did not attend. This was probably out of courtesy, in view of their association with the company 'taking over', but Charles James Cropper joined his colleagues for the group photograph (reproduced opposite) in front of the Keswick Hotel and would presumably be present at a final luncheon.

9. The glory of Lakeland's northern railway

Railwaymen and travellers prefer to forget the truncated decline of 1966-72 and remember the Keswick line's full 40 miles of active service to the community, in its magnificent setting. So in this final pictorial chapter we will celebrate this marvellous country railway, which was once such an important part of Lakeland life. The pictures have been chosen to illustrate the splendid surroundings, the characteristic motive power and distinctive traffic.

Admirers of this railway paid their last respects to the entire through route on 2 April 1966, a fortnight before closure west of Keswick, when the Stephenson Locomotive Society's North Western Area, jointly with the Manchester Locomotive Society, arranged the 'Lakes and Fells' railtour. Scenes from that memorable day are presented as a tribute to the railway and its people. The train originated in Manchester and travelled north via the Settle & Carlisle route and Carlisle Upperby to reach Penrith. Appropriately, Ivatt Class '2MT' 2-6-0s Nos 46458 and 46466 took over at this point from LNER Class 'A3' 'Pacific' No 4472 *Flying Scotsman* at Penrith's up main line platform, to take the train forward to Workington.

The weather was crisp and cold, with a good deal of snow. It was a splendid day, albeit tinged with sadness…

The line's premier passenger duty was 'The Lakes Express', which linked Workington, via Keswick and Penrith, with London Euston and vice versa. On 4 September 1954 Ivatt '2MT' 2-6-0 No 46459 pauses at Keswick with the day's down 'Lakes'. The train was worked into Penrith by Stanier 'Princess Coronation' 4-6-2 No 46236 *City of Bradford*. The beautiful light of this September evening illuminates to advantage the glazed screen and roof of the attractive buildings. Travellers from the south are dispersing to their homes and holiday haunts. *Harold D. Bowtell*

A quite magnificent picture that superbly captures the spirit of Lakeland's northern railway. On Whit Monday in 1963 a Carlisle-Keswick train is seen approaching Keswick headed by a pair of Ivatt '2MT' 2-6-0s. The train is just crossing one of the distinctive bowstring girder bridges that helped give the route its special character. *Stephen Crook*

A pleasant scene at Keswick after 1955, when the first green-liveried DMUs were introduced into service between Workington and Penrith. The detail of the cast iron canopy is interesting to note, and a painted notice ('P-3-52') on the saw-tooth valancing seems to indicate that the station was last painted in March 1952. The train is heading for Workington, and the car nearest the camera is No M79017. *Ivor Nicholas*

'The Lakes Express' again, with very clean Ivatt 2-6-0 No 46491, a stalwart of the line, climbing past Penrith No 1 box and on to the CKPR line with the down service during 1962. The leading coaches are LMS vehicles. *Derek Cross*

Above Travelling in the opposite direction down the bank towards Penrith No 1 box is 'Mickey Mouse' 2-6-0 No 46458, heading a goods train from the limeworks at Blencow, on 26 July 1962. *Derek Cross*

Below There was snow in the fells on 2 April 1966, and '2MT' No 46432 has been out with staff clearing snow from points and other problem areas between Workington and Cockermouth. The locomotive is seen at Cockermouth returning tender first to Workington. *Ian S. Carr*

Above On the same day, 2 April 1966, the joint SLS/MLS 'Lakes and Fells' railtour ran over the entire 40 miles or so between Penrith and Workington, just a couple of weeks before the section west of Keswick closed. Here the train is awaiting departure from Penrith's down main line platform after the detaching of No 4472 *Flying Scotsman* in favour of 'Mickey Mouse' 2-6-0s Nos 46458 and 46426 for the onward journey through Lakeland. *Harold D. Bowtell*

Below The 'Lakes and Fells' train is approaching Blencow, on the initial climb from Penrith. Single-line tokens will have to be exchanged in passing through the station, the buildings of which are seen ahead. *Harold D. Bowtell*

The only halt for the 'Lakes and Fells' railtour was at Keswick, looking remarkably smart and tidy at this time, despite its imminent loss of through station status. *Harold D. Bowtell*

Above With snow-capped peaks in the background, the railtour is seen hastening beside Bassenthwaite Lake, nearing Hursthole Point and Beck Wythop cottages. *Derek Cross*

Below Easing to run cautiously past Cockermouth signal box, the token authorising travel from Bassenthwaite Lake station is about to be passed out to the signalman by the fireman aboard No 46426. *Ian S. Carr*

The changeover has been effected and the new token authorising onward running to Brigham is checked by the enginemen as they accelerate through Cockermouth's platforms before carefully descending the bank to the old Cockermouth Junction and the 'C&W' section. Compare this picture with that of No 46432 (page 150) taken earlier in the day – the bright sun has completely thawed the snow that had prompted line clearance operations! Beyond Workington the railtour ran south over the former Furness main line to Hellifield and Manchester with a complement of travellers from many parts of Britain. *Flying Scotsman* took over the train again at Arnside, later that evening. *Ian S. Carr*

Acknowledgements and sources

It has been a pleasure and privilege to enjoy the co-operation of many old and new friends in the course of my research and in furthering the presentation of the story of the cross-country railway through Lakeland. The archives staff at Carlisle Castle have been ever-patient and the WCML has become well-worn in the course of 'day trips' of more than 500 miles between Oxenholme and Kew Gardens, for delvings in the Public Record Office. Above all, I thank the many folk who devoted their working lives to the railway concerned, or lived and maybe farmed beside it and then talked with me; clarity of recollection provides a wonderful perspective for the historian. I thank, among others:

Jim Airey and Mrs Airey, Frank Alcock, Roy Anderson, Doctor Michael Andrews, G. J. Aston, Nancy Banks-Smith, Mrs Bennett, J. S. Berry, Ian Bishop (and Trust House Forte, for whom he is a manager), Robert Bond, George Bott, Alan Bottomley, W. E. Boyd, J. Bernard Bradbury, Henry and Mrs Briggs, Derek J. W. Brough, Joe W. Brownrigg, Dorothy Butcher, Ian S. Carr, Joseph C. Carruthers and Mrs Elizabeth Carruthers (nee Longcake), Oliver F. Carter, John McG. Charters, Les G. Charlton, Frank Clarkson, J. G. Coates, Edgar Corless, Elizabeth Cook, Mary Cowperthwaite, Bert and Mrs Cowperthwaite, Derek Cross, E. Lloyd Daniels (and the Derwent Railway Society), J. D. Darby, W. B. Darnell, John Dawson, Alan G. Dunbar, John Duncan, Hugh G. Ellison, John Farrer, Gordon and Mrs Ferries, Neville Fields, Edward Foster, Richard D. Foster, E. H. Fowkes, Gregory R. Fox, Mrs. Emily Gates, Gordon Graham, Jack Hall, John M. Hammond, Eric W. Hannan, Kenneth Harper, Stanley and Mrs Harrison, Tom W. Hartley, William and Mrs Hebson, Major J. W. B. Hext, J. D. Hinde, Robert Hodgson, Peter Holmes, Geoffrey O. Holt, Kenneth Hoole, Geoffrey Horsman, Philip Houldershaw, the Reverend Rodney Hughes, Roy V. Hughes MBE, T. A. Hughes, Harry Jack, Tom W. Jackson and Mrs Jackson, David Jenkinson, Mrs Mary Johnston, William and Mrs Kelt, Jack Y. Lancaster, Robert Leslie, Lance Laverick, Geoffrey Lord, Peter and Ann Los, John McCallum, R. B. Hasell McCosh, Gurney MacInnes, John Mandale, Thomas Murray, Charles Neele, Edwin K. Nelson, Gordon Nichol, Kenneth J. Norman, Cecil and Mrs Oldfield, Barbara M. Patterson, John and Mrs Pattinson, Clive Pattinson, Derek A. Pattinson, George H. Pattinson, Michael Peascod, J. D. Petty, Ronald N. Redman, Syd and Mrs Ridley, John E. Roberts, Peter W. Robinson, Miss Mary Routledge, Eric S. Russell, Ian G. Sadler, Percy and Mrs Sanderson, Carol Sarsfield-Hall, Mr and Mrs Scott, James L. Slater, David L. Smith, H. R. Stones, D. H. Stuart, Ted Talbot, Richard Tangye, Thomas Taylor, David F. Tee, Albert Tims, John Tinkler, Thomas Tinkler, Joseph and Mrs Tinnion, Ron Tinnion, Jessie Titterington, Edwin and Marina Thompson, Oswald W. Todhunter, Jack Tyson, Phoebe Wallace, A. StG. Walsh, Edward Watson, Joseph K. Watson, Joseph Watson (of Workington), D. R. Wattleworth, David R. Webb, G. D. Whitworth, James Willan, J. Banks Wivell and Mrs Wivell (nee Philipson), Bob Wren, William Young and Mrs Young (formerly Hughes).

Special thanks are due to Arthur Chambers for his encouragement, and various cartography; to Doug Rendell for his extensive and professional photographic copying and other work on my behalf; and to Ken Norman for his enthusiastic pilotage in the Richard Pattinson collection (which is in the care of the Cumbrian Railways Association). Photographers and sources of illustrations are acknowledged individually, where known to me. Friends who have read critically and most helpfully through drafts of various parts of the work are: Richard Foster, John Hammond, Kenneth Hoole, Roy Hughes, David Tee, Albert Tims and Dudley Whitworth.

Authorities consulted include the Public Record Office, Kew; the National Railway Museum Library, York (with a special word of thanks for John Edgington); the Cumbria County Record Office, Carlisle Castle (Bruce Jones and colleagues); Abbot Hall Art Gallery and Museum, Kendal (Miss Mary Burkitt and colleagues); the Fitz Museum, Keswick (Norman Gandy); Manchester Central Library (and notably Harry Horton); Tullie House Library, Carlisle (Mr Wilkinson and Mr White); the library of the Institution of Civil Engineers; Cumbria County Council (Bridges Department); the Keswick Convention (Maurice Rowlandson and colleagues); British Railways (several departments, including Robert H. Blyth and colleagues of Manchester, on signalling; the Chief Civil Engineer, LMR, and his colleagues at Preston; and Messrs Nicholson and Copeland at Workington); and John Hurst and colleagues at the *Cumberland & Westmorland Herald*, Penrith, who also readily offered the hospitality of their archives.

Works of reference

The Iron and Steel Industry of West Cumberland J. Y. Lancaster & D. R. Wattleworth, 1977

Railway Reminiscences G. P. Neele, 1904

A History of the Cockermouth, Keswick and Penrith Railway W. McGowan Gradon, 1948

The Cockermouth, Keswick and Penrith Railway – In Memoriam J. M. Hammond, 1972

Forgotten Railways of North West England John Marshall, 1981

A Regional History of the Railways: the Lake Counties David Joy, 1983

The North Eastern Railway W. W. Tomlinson, 1914

The Stainmore Railway K. Hoole, 1973

History of Cockermouth J. Bernard Bradbury

Threlkeld, Cumbria; Glimpses of Village History J. H. Vine Hall, Threlkeld, 1977

Diary of George Schollick, 1893-1928

The Chronicles of Boulton's Siding Alfred Rosling Bennett, 1927, ref pp46-47 and 264

Cumbrian Families and Heraldry Roy Huddleston & R. S. Boumphrey

Notable Cumbrians Chance

Westmorland and Cumberland Leaders Ernest Gaskell

The Impact of the Railway on the development of Keswick as a tourist resort, 1860-1914 Dissertation by Paul Richard McGloin, University of Lancaster

Register of Closed Passenger and Goods Stations C. R. Clinker, 1978, and supplements

A Biographical Dictionary of Railway Engineers John Marshall, 1978

The Railway Magazine, 1897-1984, in particular 1907 (first part), J. Thornton Burge on pp372-373; and 1921 (second part), Cecil J. Allen on pp73-80

Trains Illustrated, year 1961, Cecil J. Allen on pp598-604 & 629

Cumbria December, 1966 pp432-5 and February 1973 (W. R. Mitchell on Threlkeld)

Newsletter of the Cumbrian Railways Association, including E. Craven on locomotives of the C&WR in February 1978 p9 and October 1978 pp2-5; P. W. Robinson on the CK&PR until 1866, in July 1979 pp5-7; G. Thomlinson on early days, in August 1984 pp41-46

Newsletter of the National Trust, on Canon Rawnsley

Journal of the Stephenson Locomotive Society, especially on LNWR engine sheds, and J. W. Armstrong on Tebay (the latter in 1953, pp161-2)

The Railway Observer (RCTS), particularly in the later 1930s and subsequently on renumbering of motive power depots

Railway Junction Diagrams (of the Railway Clearing House)

Ordnance Survey map sheets to 25-inch scale, various editions

Bradshaw's Railway Timetables and *Bradshaw's Manual*, various years

Index